D0467766

SNAKE PITS,
TALKING CURES,
& MAGIC BULLETS:

A History of Mental Illness

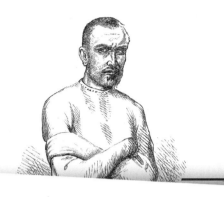

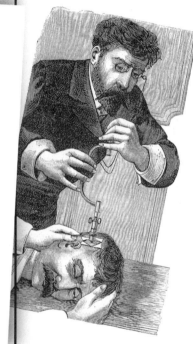

SNAKE PITS,
TALKING CURES,
& MAGIC BULLETS:

A History of Mental Illness

DEBORAH KENT

Twenty-First Century Books
Brookfield, Connecticut

For Georgia Baciu, Ruth Suratt, and Elaine Card,
teachers, guides, and helping professionals in the truest sense

Cover photograph courtesy of Mary Evans Picture Library; © Bettmann/Corbis; Culver Pictures, Inc.

Photographs courtesy of Culver Pictures, Inc.: pp. 1 (left), 56; © Bettmann/Corbis: pp. 1 (middle), 70, 100; Mary Evans Picture Library: pp. 1 (right), 23, 32, 34, 60, 80 (right), 84; Erich Lessing/Art Resource, NY: pp. 9 (Edvard Munch, 1863-1944, © ARS, NY. *The Scream*. 1893. Tempera and pastels on cardboard, 91 x 73.5 cm., National Gallery, Oslo, Norway), 30 (Hieronymus Bosch, 1450–1516. *The Ship of Fools*. Louvre, Paris, France); The Bridgeman Art Library International Ltd.: pp. 17 (Paul Kane, 1810-1871, *Medicine Mask Dance*. Oil on canvas. Royal Ontario Museum, Toronto, Canada), 20 (*Aeschylus and Hygieia*. Carved ivory relief, 5ᵗʰ century A.D.); North Wind Picture Archives: p. 41; Getty Images: pp. 50 (© Hulton/Archive), 80 (left © Archive), 127 (© Darren McCollester/Newsmakers), 135 (© Robert P. Matthews/Princeton University); © Corbis: p. 87; From *A Mind That Found Itself*: p. 93 (by Clifford Whittingham Beers, published by Longman's, Green & Co.); National Library of Medicine: p. 97 (#A010219); AP/Wide World Photos: p. 107; Photofest: p. 119; New York Public Library Picture Collection: p. 133

Published by Twenty-First Century Books
A Division of The Millbrook Press, Inc.
2 Old New Milford Road
Brookfield, CT 06804

Library of Congress Cataloging-in-Publication Data
Kent, Deborah.
Snake pits, talking cures, and magic bullets: a history of mental illness/Deborah Kent.
p. cm.
Includes bibliographical references and index.
Summary: Looks at how the mentally ill have been treated throughout history, focusing on advances made in the 19th and 20th centuries regarding mental hospitals, medications, and social acceptance.
ISBN 0-7613-2704-5
1. Mental illness—History—Juvenile literature.
[1. Mental illness.]   I. Title.
RC438.K46 2003
616.89'009—dc21   2002011208

Text copyright © 2003 by Deborah Kent
Printed in the United States of America
All rights reserved
5 4 3 2 1

•CONTENTS•

#26.00

millbrook/Bondi

12/16/03

LIBRARY
DEXTER SCHOOLS
DEXTER, NM 88230

Chapter One

ONE
OUT OF
FOUR

Long Island experienced an unseasonal heat wave in May of 1991, and Stan Gunter's apartment was stifling. Stan couldn't concentrate on the song he was trying to compose. He opened a book, hoping to study Spanish grammar, but the words were a meaningless blur. In search of relief, Stan stepped onto his fourth-floor balcony.

  The heat was unbearable, but it was not the only cause of Stan's distress. For several weeks strange voices had filled his head. Sometimes they praised him, and at other times they scolded and taunted. At first he didn't know who was talking to him, though he was sure the voices carried a crucial message. Now at last everything had become clear.

Stan was certain that the high, light voice belonged to Jesus Christ. The deep, commanding voice came from God Himself.

In a dreamlike haze Stan Gunter sat on the balcony, absorbed by the conversation that clamored through his mind. Jesus and God began to argue. They were going to go to war, one against the other, and the whole world would be destroyed. There was only one way to spare humankind, the voices explained. He, Stan Gunter, must sacrifice his life. He must die to save the rest of humanity.

Stan thought of the people who loved him—his friends, his parents, his fiancée. He knew they would grieve over his death. But the world was in danger. He had no choice. Climbing onto a chair, he leaped from the balcony and crashed to the concrete parking lot 35 feet (11 meters) below.

A downstairs neighbor saw Stan's body hurtle past her window, and rushed to call an ambulance. When Stan reached the hospital he was barely alive. His injuries were appalling. His nose was shattered, and he had multiple fractures of his arms and legs. Many of his internal organs were badly bruised, and he was in shock. Most dangerous of all, his aorta had ruptured. The aorta is the main artery that carries blood from the heart. Without immediate surgery, Stan would have died from internal hemorrhaging.

Miraculously Stan survived the emergency surgery and began to improve. But over the next few weeks his condition remained critical. Twice he nearly died from raging infections. Each time he pulled through with the help of the medical team.

Stan Gunter's troubles had begun twelve years earlier when, at the age of twenty-four, he heard voices for the first time. They threatened him with dire punishment unless he practiced the piano without stopping. He played almost constantly, not daring to sleep or eat. At last his family took him to a hospital, where

WHAT IS SCHIZOPHRENIA?

Schizophrenia is one of the most severe forms of mental illness. It usually begins in the teens or early twenties, and may be a lifelong disability. Symptoms of schizophrenia include confused, disorganized thinking and loss of contact with reality. The person may imagine that he is being persecuted, or may hear voices no one else can hear. People with schizophrenia often have trouble relating to others, and tend to become withdrawn and isolated.

This classic painting of mental torment is entitled The Scream. *It was painted by Edvard Munch (1863-1944), who himself suffered from mental instability.*

doctors concluded he had a mental illness called schizophrenia. They prescribed medications to control his symptoms, and recommended counseling to help him deal with his condition.

After his first hospitalization Stan improved dramatically. But in the years that followed, his illness surfaced time after time. When he was well Stan held a job as a translator. He played the piano for his friends, and mastered several additional foreign languages. But then, unpredictably, his illness overwhelmed him. Reality faded, swept aside by the fears and fantasies that came to life inside his head.

When Stan Gunter was finally on the mend after his leap from the balcony, his doctors called in a psychiatrist for a consultation. The medical team hoped for a treatment plan that would conquer Stan's illness and keep him from making further suicide attempts. But the psychiatrist felt Stan was already on the best possible course of medication. Maybe Stan would improve, but there was no guarantee. Most likely he would be tormented by voices yet again. "We spent a couple of months putting him back together," said one of Stan's surgeons, "and if you think about it, we never fixed the cause of his problem."[1]

The science of medicine made astounding progress during the twentieth century. In the developed nations, most contagious diseases were brought under control with antibiotics, immunizations, and improved sanitary conditions. Highly sophisticated tests and treatments aided in the fight against cancer, heart disease, diabetes, and other chronic illnesses. Researchers even began to unlock the secrets of human genetics, opening a promising new field of treatment and prevention.

While medicine accomplished miracles in the care of the physically ill, illnesses of the mind largely remained a mystery. One after another, new treatment methods were heralded as breakthroughs. Yet each new method proved to have limitations, and none provided the dreamed-of cure.

In 2001 the World Health Organization (WHO) estimated that one person in every four worldwide will experience a mental disorder at some period during his or her lifetime. Studies in the United States show that between 1 and 2 percent of the population will develop schizophrenia, and some 20 percent will experience a major depression. Mental illness may emerge at any point during the life cycle, from early childhood to old age, and it strikes both rich and poor. Among the conditions regarded as mental illnesses are schizophrenia, depression, bipolar or manic-

THE TERRIBLE PRICE

In 1997 the National Institute of Mental Health (NIMH) estimated that American taxpayers and consumers spend approximately $200 billion a year on drugs, therapies, and hospital stays to treat mental disorders. The cost of mental illness jumps to $300 billion annually when we factor in the lost wages of patients and their relatives who act as caregivers. In addition to the economic toll, mental illness can be deadly. Though studies vary, it is estimated that about one in ten people with schizophrenia eventually commit suicide. The figure is even higher for people who have major depression—about 15 percent die by their own hands.

depressive disorder, post-traumatic stress disorder, Alzheimer's disease, and dependence on drugs or alcohol. Though these conditions differ dramatically, they all affect a person's emotions and behavior. They may hinder an individual from working, making friends, getting along with family members, enjoying hobbies, traveling, or even meeting basic needs such as eating, dressing, and bathing.

Sooner or later nearly every family is touched by the mental illness of one or more of its members. If you were to survey a group of your friends, you might discover that Sarah's father has a drinking problem, Jenny's grandmother lives in an Alzheimer's unit in a nursing home, Pete's aunt takes antidepressant medication, and Brandon's sister was hospitalized for three months due to schizophrenia. Yet, though mental illness is widespread, it triggers deep-seated fears in those regarded as "well." We expect people to behave within certain norms—to control their anger, excitement, and sadness; to dress like others of their age and social status; to behave more or less the way others behave around them. Because people who are mentally ill may speak or act in strange ways, we tend to fear, ridicule, and shun them. Rose Tomkins, a Boston woman who was hospitalized numerous times for severe depression, suggests that we fear in others what we sometimes glimpse in ourselves. "I think . . . we all have these demons," Rose explained in an interview. "What I think madness is—[the demons] act out more in some of us."[2]

Because mental illness makes us so uncomfortable, we often try to distance ourselves from the mentally ill. We refer to them with a host of demeaning words and phrases. We describe someone with extreme behavior as "nuts," "loony," "crazy," "deranged," "demented," "touched in the head," "certifiable," or "out to lunch." We make knowing gestures and roll our eyes to suggest that someone is "off his rocker." "Her elevator doesn't go all the way to the top," we say, laughing uneasily. "He's a few cards short of a deck," we giggle. "She's not wrapped too tight." When we label another person in this way, we assure ourselves that we, at least, are sane and solid.

What exactly are the mental illnesses that fill us with such anxiety and dread? People have debated the nature of madness throughout history, and have struggled to unravel its complex causes. Doctors, philosophers, philanthropists, and ordinary citizens have offered theories and experimented with treatments. People with mental illness have been seen as dangerous or blessed, as harmless fools or threats to society. They have been tortured, chained, banished, exhibited as freaks, and burned at the stake. The most widely held view today likens disorders of the mind to illnesses of the body. Within this framework psychiatrists diagnose the patient's disease and prescribe medications and other therapies.

Our questions about the nature of mental illness have changed over time, but the debate has never ceased. Is mental

M. I. AND M. R.

During the twentieth century many state-run institutions were divided into two major sections, labeled M.I. (mentally ill) and M.R. (mentally retarded). Both mental illness and mental retardation affect the mind, but they are radically different conditions. Mental illnesses involve disordered thought processes and emotions that run out of control. Mental retardation is a matter of low intelligence, ranging from mild to profound. A person who is mentally ill may have average, below average, or even soaring intelligence. By the same token, a person with mental retardation may be mentally healthy; regardless of her disability she may have fulfilling work and interests, rewarding relationships with friends and family, and positive feelings about herself. Mental illness and mental retardation can also occur simultaneously, as some people with retardation also develop mental illnesses.

There are many overlaps between the history of mental illness and the history of mental retardation. Like the mentally ill, people with retardation have been abused, shunned, taunted, and segregated in institutions. Like the mentally ill, they are struggling to find greater acceptance within the community. But the histories of these two conditions are also very different. This is not a book about mental retardation. Instead it will focus on our understanding of mental illness through the ages and our treatment of people considered mentally ill.

illness triggered by the events in our lives, or is it programmed into our genetic makeup? Is it the result of some chemical imbalance in the brain? Can its effects be softened by talking to a therapist? Can healthy behavior be learned, and unhealthy patterns be unlearned? Some spokespersons for psychiatric patients challenge the very concept of "mental illness." They argue that emotional turmoil, however severe, is an understandable reaction to a frightening, tumultuous world.

To label a group of people as "mentally ill" measures them against a majority assumed to be "normal." Yet each of us, at times, feels overwhelmed by anger or sadness, by unbounded elation or unaccountable fear. Nearly all of us can remember moments when we ask ourselves, "Can this be real? Am I imagining it? Do I really understand what I think just happened to me?" Who then is mad? And is anyone truly and unshakably sane?

In the late 1600s an English playwright named Nathaniel Lee asked the same questions as he was locked up in a London asylum. "I called them mad, and they called me mad," he wrote, "and damn them—they outvoted me!"[3]

Chapter Two

DEMONS OF THE ANCIENTS

And they came over unto the other side of the sea, into the country of the Gadarenes. And when He was come out of the ship, immediately there met Him out of the tombs a man with an unclean spirit, who had his dwelling among the tombs; and no man could bind him, no, not with chains: Because that he had been often bound with fetters and chains, and the chains had been plucked asunder by him, and the fetters broken in pieces: neither could any man tame him. And always, night and day, he was in the mountains, and in the tombs, crying, and cutting himself with stones.

— The Gospel According to Mark, Chapter 5.

THE SHAMAN'S ART

"That guy's sure got the devil in him!" we exclaim sometimes when we see someone raging and threatening bodily harm. We don't literally believe that the person is possessed by demons. Nevertheless, we borrow a phrase that meant something very real to our ancestors. When people believed that the world was inhabited by a multitude of spirits—some benign and some dangerous—demonic possession seemed a logical way to explain bizarre behavior.

We have no way of knowing whether mental illnesses affected human beings in prehistoric times. However, anthropologists have found mentally disturbed people among most of the preindustrial groups they have visited in the past two centuries. Some Native North Americans referred to madness as "loss of the soul" or being "lost to oneself." These descriptions suggest that the mad person has somehow lost the very essence of his or her personality, entering an altered state or even becoming a different person. Such soul loss was thought to occur in two ways. The spirits might be punishing the afflicted person for violating a tribal law or taboo. In other cases, madness could be inflicted through magical powers by one of the person's enemies.

Native North American healers, or shamans, treated a wide range of illnesses, including disorders of the mind. The shaman was thought to be in direct communication with the supernatural

PSYCHOSURGERY IN THE STONE AGE

Human skulls from the Neolithic period, or Stone Age, occasionally bear tiny holes which were apparently drilled with a small, sharp tool. Modern physicians sometimes use this procedure, known as trepanning, to relieve pressure on the brain. No one knows for certain why trepanning was practiced by our ancestors. Archaeologists suspect that early humans used this technique to release the demons which they believed were causing a person's madness.

*This painting shows Native North American shamans wearing the
fantastical masks they used in their healing ceremonies.*

spirits. Usually the shaman performed a cleansing ritual
intended to purify the person who was ill. If the breaking of a
taboo was suspected, the person would be called upon to make
a full confession. By leading the mad person to confess and purg-
ing him of evil spirits, the shaman hoped to bring about a cure.

If madness resulted from magic—if the person had been
cursed by an enemy—the shaman treated it differently. In such
cases the person was thought to be afflicted by an evil spirit or

demon that had entered his body. Rituals were designed to rid him of this tormenting spirit. After chanting and dancing the shaman might remove a toad, snake, or venomous insect from the ill person's body. Though the creature was invisible to everyone else, the shaman claimed to see it and dispose of it.

Shamanic practices illustrate the tremendous impact of belief upon groups and individuals. In a society where people believe in powerful unseen spirits, spirit possession seems to be a reasonable way to explain disordered thinking and behavior. If an illness is caused by the invasion of an evil spirit, then the exorcism, or ritual removal of such a spirit, can bring about a cure. Shamans may be effective through the "power of suggestion"—that is, they heal the sick because patients believe their rituals will be effective. Through the shaman's chants and dances, the lost soul is restored to the body.

DEMONS AND DEITIES

About four thousand years ago the Babylonians of the Tigris-Euphrates Valley (present-day Iraq) developed a form of writing known as *cuneiform*. By deciphering the cuneiform symbols on ancient clay tablets, scholars have made fascinating discoveries about Babylonian beliefs and healing practices. The Babylonian belief system included a host of demons, each one responsible for a particular illness. Healing required a correct "diagnosis" of the illness, in order for the priests to perform the proper rituals to appease the demon in question. Insanity was caused by a demon called Idta. One Babylonian tablet is inscribed with a "prescription" for treating mental illness: "Take a bucket. Fill it with water from the mouth of the river. Impart to this the exalted magic power. Sprinkle the man with it. May insanity be dispelled!"[1]

Like the shamans of preliterate societies, priests in ancient Egypt practiced rituals for healing the body and the mind.

Egyptian priests treated troubled persons by inducing an "incubation sleep," probably through the use of opium or a similar drug. In this drug-induced state the patient had strange dreams, which he later described to a priest. The priest interpreted these dreams for the patient, explaining the cause of his illness and its further course of treatment.

THE FIRST ASYLUMS

Ancient Sanskrit records show that Hindu physicians in India established shelters, or asylums, for mentally ill persons in about 1400 B.C. These early doctors wrote that disturbed persons should be treated with kindness and understanding.

In magnificent temples dedicated to the healing god Asklepios (also known as Aesculapius), priests of ancient Greece performed a variety of rituals for the cure of physically and mentally ill persons. The priests also served as gatekeepers, deciding which patients would be admitted to the temple for treatment. The sickest and poorest people who came to the temple were often turned away.

A patient accepted for treatment at an Aesculapian temple first underwent a series of cleansing procedures. He was given drugs to purge his digestive tract. Later he bathed in the sacred spring at the center of the temple courtyard. After the bath he received a massage to relax his muscles. Properly purified, he was ready for the next step—an incubation sleep and its accompanying dreams.

The practice of inducing incubation sleep came to the Greeks from ancient Egypt. Because records from ancient Greece are quite extensive, we have a vivid picture of how these incubation procedures were conducted. A priest gave the patient a goblet containing a sleep-inducing drink, and led him, half-dazed, through the corridors of an underground labyrinth. At last they reached a sleeping chamber, or *abaton*, where the patient lay down on a pallet and fell into a trancelike state. In this state the patient saw visions and heard the voice of the god

Asklepios himself. Sometimes the god's words were enough to bring about the patient's cure. At other times the god gave instructions for the patient's treatment, which were then interpreted and carried out by the temple priests.

The rituals of the priests were closely guarded secrets, and no one knows for certain what really went on in the incubation chambers. Many scholars believe that the priests used some form of ventriloquism to create the god's voice. In his drugged state, the patient was probably very suggestible—that is, he expected to meet a god, so he readily believed that the strange, hollow voice he heard came from the god's mouth.

Often Asklepios prescribed treatments involving snakes. Under the god's direction, a priest would place a live snake on a

THE POWER OF THE SERPENT

Since the days of ancient Greece, the snake has had deep symbolic meaning for physicians. As the snake sheds its worn-out skin and emerges fresh and clean, so the physician hopes to help the patient emerge from his illness, renewed and restored to health. The Aesculapian staff, a stick entwined with a snake, still appears on medical diplomas today.

Carved ivory bas relief friezes of Aesculapius, the Roman god of medicine and healing, and Hygieia, the Greek goddess of health.

patient's arms or legs. One temple, at Delphi, contained a large pit filled with hissing, writhing serpents. The patient was suspended above this pit as a cure for his madness. It was believed that the shock of this experience would jolt the patient back to his senses.[2] Somehow an encounter that might drive a sane person mad was thought capable of driving a mad person back to sanity.

THE MIND AND THE BODY

While the priests performed their rituals in the healing temples, Greek physicians and philosophers questioned belief in sacred incantations and divine powers. Instead they sought to understand illness and healing by unraveling the mysteries of the human body. The philosopher Plato (428–348 B.C.) concluded that the brain was the seat of the higher moral qualities, which he called the "rational soul." This rational soul was immortal and godlike, the very best and purest in human nature. The "irrational soul," on the other hand, was located in the chest. It governed the baser emotions, such as anger, fear, lust, and jealousy. No doubt Plato connected the heart with intense emotion because of the way it pounds and races when we are excited or upset.

Plato believed that disturbance of the mind came from three possible causes—disease of the body, an imbalance of base emotions, or intervention by the gods. His writings describe several conditions which are considered mental illnesses today. He wrote about melancholia, or depression—a condition in which a person seems to lose all interest in life. He also described manic states, in which a person becomes wildly euphoric or uncontrollably agitated. Plato thought that these conditions developed when the base emotions clamored to express themselves and overwhelmed the rational soul. He argued that such conditions should be treated not by the priests with their snakes and chanting, but by philosophers who used the powers of persuasion. By talking to the patient—exhorting him to act rationally, threatening him with confinement, or promising rewards for good behavior—the philosopher/physician could help the patient bring his unruly emotions under control.

Though Plato drew a clear distinction between the mind and the body, he understood that the two were inexorably linked. "If the head and body are to be well, you must begin by curing the soul," he wrote. "That is the first thing."[3] Plato's notions about mind and body have endured in Western thought to the present time.

Plato's treatment plan for the mentally ill aimed to restore the patient's mind and body to order and harmony. In a wider sense, Plato was concerned with order and harmony in society as a whole. The disruptive, unpredictable behavior of persons with mental illness threatened the peace of the community. Plato suggested a law to protect the citizens of Athens from deranged persons who lived in their midst: "If a man is mad he shall not be at large in the city, but his family shall keep him at home in any way which they can, or if not, let them pay a penalty."[4]

The Greek physician Hippocrates (c. 460–377 B.C.) suggested that mental illness was triggered by an imbalance of humors in the body. According to Greek medical lore, the body contained four humors, or vital substances: black bile, yellow bile, phlegm, and blood. Each of these humors corresponded to one of the four basic elements thought to compose the universe: black bile to earth, yellow bile to fire, phlegm to water, and blood to air. Too much earth, or black bile, caused the sufferer to have a melancholy temperament. If a person had too much yellow bile, the fire humor, he might be excessively angry and passionate. Phlegm, being cold and moist like water, caused sluggishness. An excess of blood, in contrast, gave a florid complexion and a cheerful, robust personality.

*A sixteenth-century woodcut illustrating the ancient
Greek theory of the four humors.*

Hippocrates proposed various remedies to bring the humors into proper balance. If a patient was melancholy, he recommended ridding the body of black bile through the use of hellebore, an herb to induce vomiting. Following these treatments he recommended building up the supply of blood with plenty of good food and exercise.

While Plato argued that human emotions were based in the heart, Hippocrates recognized the central role of the brain in our feeling states:

> Men ought to know that from the brain, and from the brain only, arise our pleasures, joys, laughter and jests, as well as our sorrows, pains, griefs, and tears. Through it in particular we think, see, hear, and distinguish the beautiful from the ugly, the bad from the good, the pleasant from the unpleasant. . . . It is the same thing which makes us mad or delirious, inspires us with dread and fear whether by night or by day, brings sleeplessness, inopportune mistakes, aimless anxieties, absent-mindedness, and acts that are contrary to habit. These things that we suffer all come from the brain when it is not healthy, but becomes abnormally hot, cold, moist, or dry. . . . Madness comes from its moistness.[5]

Claudius Galen (A.D. 129–216), a Greek physician who practiced in the Roman Empire, accepted the theory of humors but also made a close study of human anatomy by dissecting cadavers. His investigations led him to believe that a network of nerves carried messages and sensations to and from every part of the body. The brain, Galen wrote, was the center of this vast nervous system. Galen completely renounced the influence of the gods in causing disease, including diseases of the mind. "Do not go to the gods to make inquiries and thus attempt by soothsaying to discover the nature of the directing soul," he wrote, ". . . but go and take instruction from an anatomist."[6]

The ideas of the great Greek philosophers did not generally filter down to the common people. Only a handful of people in the ancient world could read and write, and the poor and uneducated held an assortment of superstitious beliefs about everything from crops and the weather to diseases of the body and the mind. They attributed madness to witchcraft, possession, or the anger of the gods. Mad persons were feared and despised. They were laughed at, chained up, stoned, or driven out of their villages.

The story of the Gadarene in the New Testament Book of Mark is a clear example of how madness was perceived on the fringes of the Roman Empire at the dawn of the Christian Era. In this story villagers attempt to bind a highly agitated man with chains, but with superhuman strength he breaks free and flees to the mountains. He exhibits what mental-health workers today would call "self-mutilating behavior," cutting himself with stones. According to Mark, this man is possessed by "an unclean spirit." When Jesus speaks to him, a legion of devils replies from within the man's body. Jesus drives out these devils, which enter the bodies of pigs and rush into the sea. As soon as the devils have left him the man becomes peaceful and rational.

During the first centuries of the Christian Era, the newly formed church swept aside the ideas of the Greek philosopher/physicians. The church denounced scientific study, and strictly forbade the dissection of cadavers. Though folk medicine continued to flourish, the church claimed that faith was the only true road to healing. Once again, as they had in Babylonia, Egypt, and Greece, priests took charge of the healing arts.

LIGHT IN THE DARK AGES

European science lay dormant throughout the long medieval period, often referred to as the Dark Ages (A.D. 500–1300). Meanwhile, physicians in the Middle East carried forward the medical inquiries that began in ancient Greece. They embraced the ideas of the Greek physicians, and worked them into a growing body of knowledge about mental diseases. Arab doctors became highly sophisticated in their classification of various mental disorders. Unhammad, a Persian physician of the ninth century A.D., described nine major kinds of mental illness, each divided into numerous subtypes. Among these illnesses was *kutrib*, a condition in which a person imagines that he is being persecuted by others. By its description, *kutrib* sounds very much like the condition we call paranoia today. Unhammad's *murrae souda* resembles the condition known today as obsessive-compulsive disorder (OCD). A person with *murrae souda* was plagued with groundless worries and the uncontrollable need to carry out certain repetitive behaviors, such as touching door-frames or counting floor tiles.

Another famous physician of the Islamic world was Abu Al-Husayn ibn Sina (980–1037) of Persia. To Europeans Ibn Sina became known as Avicenna. Avicenna compiled a detailed medical encyclopedia describing a wide variety of diseases, including a number of mental illnesses. Like Plato, Avicenna renounced the notion that mental disturbance was caused by evil spirits—the djinns of Arabic mythology. Instead he accepted Hippocrates idea that illness of the mind sprang from imbalances of the body's humors. Among the conditions Avicenna listed in his encyclopedia were depression, mania, and "lovesickness."

One of the greatest physicians of the medieval period was Moses Ben Maimon, or Maimonides (1135–1204), who studied and practiced at the royal court in Cairo, Egypt. Maimonides wrote in Arabic, though his own background was Jewish. He had many ideas about mental illnesses, which he regarded as "diseases of the soul." Like Avicenna, Maimonides understood that emotional upheaval can cause physical changes in the body.

He also accepted Plato's notion that human beings have an innate moral sense. In some cases of mental disturbance, this

THE LOVESICK PRINCE

According to a Persian legend, the king once ordered Avicenna to attend his nephew, who was stricken with a mysterious malady. He lay on his bed, too despondent to move. After talking with the young man, Avicenna was convinced that he suffered from lovesickness. But the king's nephew refused to disclose who was the object of his affection. Avicenna rested his finger lightly on the patient's wrist, where he could feel his beating pulse. Then he named all of the districts in the city. At one particular name, the sick man's pulse fluttered noticeably. Avicenna then listed all of the streets in that district, until he felt another telltale flutter. Finally Avicenna listed all of the houses on the street in question. When the pulse fluttered again, he knew the house where the young man's sweetheart lived. Avicenna took this information to the king and urged him to arrange his nephew's marriage to the girl he loved. The king agreed, and the young man's lovesickness was cured.

A principle similar to the one Avicenna used in this story is employed in the modern polygraph, or lie-detector, test. The polygraph measures the galvanic skin response, the tendency of the hands to sweat in stressful situations, as when a person tells an untruth. The quickening pulse and the sweating palms are both measurable physical responses to mental excitement.

moral sense is thrown out of balance. As Maimonides explained, "The wicked and the morally perverted imagine that the bad is good and the good is bad."[7]

Meanwhile, in Europe, the Catholic Church was on its own relentless mission to separate good from evil. Those who were deemed to be mad often found themselves at the mercy of religious and political forces as devastating as the illness that haunted their lives.

Chapter Three

SAINTS AND WITCHES

It has indeed lately come to our ears, not without inflicting us with bitter sorrow, that in some parts of northern Germany, as well as in the provinces, townships, territories, and dioceses of Mainz, Cologne, Salzburg, and Bremen, many persons of both sexes, unmindful of their own salvation and straying from the Catholic faith, have abandoned themselves to evil, incubi, succubi, and their incantations, spells, conjurations, and their other accursed charms and crafts, . . . have blasted produce of the earth, [and] afflict and torment men and women.

— From the Bull of
Pope Innocent VIII, 1484

BEYOND THE WALLS

During the Middle Ages in Europe, most towns and cities were surrounded by walls as protection against invaders. At night the city gates creaked shut, bolting solid citizens safely inside, and locking potential enemies out. The town watchmen tried to drive all undesirables outside the walls. Such undesirables included beggars, lepers, and madmen.

Since madness was equated with demonic possession or witchcraft, most people were deeply afraid of people with mental disturbances. Often, however, this fear expressed itself in mockery. The village madman was an object of ridicule. Children followed him through the streets, taunting him and pelting him with stones. Their elders cheered them on, and sometimes joined in the chase, brandishing sticks and whips. Sooner or later, the madman would be chased out of the village. Shakespeare describes one such unfortunate soul, Poor Tom, in *King Lear*, forced to fend for himself in the woods and fields.

Poor Tom; that eats the swimming frog, the toad,
The tadpole, the wall-newt and the water;
That in the fury of his heart, when the foul fiend rages,
Eats cow-dung for sallets; swallows the old rat and the
   ditch-dog;
Drinks the green mantle of the standing pool;
Who is whipped from tithing to tithing,
And stock-punished, and imprisoned;
Who hath had three suits to his back, six shirts to his
   body,
Horse to ride, and weapon to wear;
But mice and rats, and such small fare,
Have been Tom's food for seven long year.[1]

Hieronymous Bosch (1450-1516) was an eccentric painter and allegorist. He took the idea of a ship of fools and turned it into one of his most famous paintings, entitled The Ship of Fools. *Bosch places in the ship representatives of humanity who appear to be happily idle on a ship going nowhere.*

In many port cities, ships' captains were paid to remove a mad person to some safely distant town. Records in Frankfurt, Germany, suggest that this was a common practice in the late fourteenth and early fifteenth centuries. Documents describe a madman who was shipped out of the city in 1399 after he ran naked through the streets. In another case, a mad blacksmith was shipped out, but the captain cheated the city fathers and set him ashore only a few miles away. The blacksmith made his way back to Frankfurt, but the city was determined to be rid of him. He was sent off on yet another ship, and this time he never returned. The notion of the "ship of fools," laden with insane men and women, has captured the imaginations of painters and poets for centuries.

Some people with mental illness fared better. If a disturbed woman or man came from a loving family, she or he would be protected as much as possible. Aristocratic families had the means to shelter a mad uncle or sister within a castle turret. They might seek treatment for their agitated relative by taking him to a priest. They might engage a physician who had dabbled in the writings of Hippocrates and Galen, and prescribed herbs to balance the patient's humors. Poorer folk sought help from "old wives," women who blended superstition and a traditional knowledge of herbs to offer prescriptions for a wide assortment of ills. One such cure was recorded in *The Leech Book of Blad*, a collection of folk remedies compiled in England sometime in the eleventh century:

> When a devil possess a man or controls him from within
> with disease, [give] a spew drink [to cause vomiting] of
> lupine, bishopwort, and henbane. Pound these together.
> Add ale for a liquid. Let it stand for a night. Add cathartic
> grains and holy water, to be drunk out of a church bell.[2]

THE MADNESS OF SIR LANCELOT

In *Le Morte d'Arthur* (first printed in 1485), Sir Thomas Malory chronicles the legends of King Arthur and his Knights of the Round Table. In one of these tales, the noble Sir Lancelot falls prey to an evil enchantment that causes him to go mad. A fellow knight finds him wandering in the forest, filthy and half-starved, and leads him to the castle, where "they bound his hands and his feet, and gave him good meals and good drink, and brought him back again to his strength and his fairness. But in his wits they could not bring him again, nor to know himself." After a year and a half, Lancelot breaks free and wanders into a village, where "all the young men of the city ran after him, and there they strew turf at him, and gave him many said strokes, and as Sir Lancelot might reach any of them he threw them so that they would nevermore come into his hands. For of some he break their legs, and some their arms, and so fled into the castle." Lancelot is finally cured of his madness when the enchantment is lifted.[3]

The famous painter N.C. Wyeth illustrated a 1927 book called The Boy's King Arthur. *This is his portrait of Lancelot in the throes of madness.*

On occasion the friends and family of a highly agitated person would use physical restraint to keep him or her under control. Eventually some people grew calm and could be set free.

THE POWER OF THE CHURCH

In a medieval village, everyone understood the language of the church bells. There was the early-morning call to Mass, which the most faithful heeded not only on Sundays, but on weekdays as well. There was the clangor of alarm in cases of fire or enemy attack. There were the joyous peals of wedding bells, and the solemn tones of the death knell when one of the villagers died. Like radio, television, and the Internet today, the church bells carried news and told people what to do.

The bells were the ever-present voice of the Roman Catholic Church, the most powerful body in Western Europe. Kingdoms rose and fell, rulers came and vanished, but the church remained immovable. For most Europeans it was the supreme authority. It told them when to pray, when to celebrate, when to mourn. Most of all, the church told its followers what to believe.

For the medieval peasant, life was full of fears and uncertainties. Droughts and storms could ruin his crops. Disease could kill his children overnight. But even though life on Earth was brutally hard, the church assured him that an eternal reward awaited him in heaven. If he was faithful and obedient in this world, he would know rapture in the next. But if he was rebellious, if he disobeyed the warnings of the priests, he would suffer forever the agonies of hellfire.

According to the church the world was a constant battleground between the forces of good and evil. The forces of good belonged to God and His son Jesus Christ. Their assistants in the fight were the saints and angels. On the side of evil were Satan and his legions of lesser devils. It was essential for all

LIBRARY
DEXTER SCHOOLS
DEXTER, NM 88230

Christians to align themselves with the good by adhering strictly to the church's doctrines.

The ancient belief that demons can enter a person's body was alive and well in medieval Europe. If a person became agitated and spoke wildly, most people suspected demonic possession rather than some form of natural illness. Since the disturbance was caused by demons, the best person to treat it was a priest. Priests sometimes treated ill or agitated persons through the application of holy relics. A relic was any object reputed to have been touched by Jesus Christ or one of the saints. The sale of holy relics was big business in medieval Europe. It has been said that by the end of the Middle Ages European churches contained enough splinters from the True Cross to fill an entire forest. Nails from the Cross, laces from Christ's sandals, or bits of His clothing appeared in churches all over Europe. A lock of a saint's hair, brushed over the head of a madwoman or man, was thought to have miraculous healing powers.

A piece of the "True Cross" is encased in the center rectangle and surrounded by pearls and semi-precious stones in this sixth-century relic.

Another form of healing, the exorcism, bears an uncanny resemblance to rituals performed by shamans in many parts of the world. In both instances, a religious healer carries out a ritual to drive a demon from the body of the possessed. The Catholic Church specified a series of rituals that a priest should follow, step by step, in cases of possession by the devil. First the priest prayed alone. He called upon God to give him strength with which to face Satan's power. Then the priest went to the person undergoing the exorcism, and chanted: "In the name of Him who rules the seas and the winds, the heavens and the earth! In the name of Him who was crucified by men! May the Devil, the adversary of all, leave the body of the possessed and return to the regions from whence he came!"[4] At last the priest touched a crucifix to the forehead of the pos-

BACK TO TREPANNING

A thirteenth-century physician, Arnald de Villanova (1235–1313), recommended a treatment reminiscent of the trepanning practiced in preliterate societies. If a person was in a frenzied or manic state, de Villanova suggested carving a cross into the top of his skull. Both demons and excess humors could escape through the hole.

sessed person, then to the heart, and finally to the forehead again. At this point the demon was supposed to emerge from the body of the possessed person. Many medieval paintings depict ghoulish forms emerging from the mouths or bodies of anguished sufferers.

In some instances, strange and unpredictable behavior was regarded in quite a different way. If a person prayed obsessively, fasted to the point of starvation, and claimed to see visions of Jesus and Mary, she or he was thought to be in special communication with the Holy Spirit. Lukardis (?–1309), a nun from Oberweim in present-day Germany, claimed that she did not eat for months and was kept alive by nursing from Mary's breast. Today most psychiatrists would say that Lukardis had a religious delusion. But during her lifetime people believed her amazing story and held her in high esteem.

An Englishwoman named Margery Kempe (1373–1438) encountered both Christ and the devil in her tumultuous inner world. Kempe, who was herself illiterate, dictated her life story to a friend, thus leaving behind an extraordinary record. At the

THE MAID OF ORLEANS

In 1425, in the midst of the Hundred Years' War in Europe, a thirteen-year-old French peasant girl named Joan began to hear voices and see strange visions. Joan of Arc (1412?–1431) was convinced that the saints were communicating with her, urging her to free France from English rule and put the French king upon his rightful throne. She was so convincing that she rallied a following of passionate believers. In 1429 the would-be king, Charles VII, gave in to her pleading and placed her in command of an army. Amazingly, Joan led her men to victory at the city of Orleans. In 1431 Joan was captured and tried for witchcraft by the English. Though she insisted that her visions were sent by God, she was burned at the stake. She was canonized, or granted sainthood, by Pope Benedict XV in 1920.

If she heard her voices and saw her visions today, most likely Joan would be diagnosed as schizophrenic. She would be sent to a hospital and given medication to subdue her symptoms. But in fifteenth-century France, Joan was seen as a messenger from God. Which was she, in reality—a schizophrenic or a visionary leader? Or could it be that she was both at once?

age of twenty-one she nearly died giving birth to her first child, and became deeply concerned with an unconfessed sin that weighed upon her conscience. When she tried to make her confession the priest was "too hasty and began to reprove her." She could not unburden herself of her sin for fear of the priest, yet she was terrified of hellfire. As her book explains, "For the dread she had of damnation on one side, and his sharp reproving of her on the other side, this creature went out of her mind and was wondrously vexed and labored with spirits for half a year, eight weeks, and odd days."

The *Book of Margery Kempe* details experiences that would be called hallucinations by mental-health professionals today. To Kempe and those around her, they were manifestations of the forces of good and evil that dictated the world. "In this time she saw, as she thought, devils opening their mouths, all inflamed with waves of fire, as if they would have swallowed her in, pulling her and hauling her night and day. . . ." Directed by these demons:

> She slandered her husband, her friends, and herself. She said many a wicked word, and many a cruel word. . . . She would have destroyed herself many a time, . . . And also she rived the skin of her body against her heart with her nails spitefully, and worse she would have done, but that she was bound and kept with strength by day and night so that she might not have her will.[5]

After eight months of torment, Kempe was suddenly relieved by a vision of Christ standing at her bedside. The devils were banished, and she was filled with religious fervor.

> Sometimes she heard with her bodily ears such sounds and melodies that she could not well hear what a man said to her at that time unless he spoke the louder. . . . She saw with her bodily eyes many white things flying all about her on every side, as thick as specks in a sunbeam. . . . She saw them many diverse times and in many diverse places, both in church and in her chamber, at her meat and at her prayers, in the fields and in town, both going and sitting. And many times she was afraid what they might be, for she saw them as well at night in darkness as in daylight. Then when she was afraid of them Our Lord said to her, "By this token, daughter, know that it is God

HEARING VOICES, SEEING THINGS

Today when someone hears voices that no one else can hear, or sees things that other people cannot see, she or he is said to be having hallucinations. Most hallucinations are auditory. Visual, tactile, and even olfactory hallucinations can also occur, but they are quite rare. The term "hallucination" comes from Greek words meaning "to wander" or "to be distraught." Most mental-health professionals regard hallucinations to be signs of a major mental illness such as schizophrenia. They can also be triggered by drugs such as LSD.

One man, diagnosed as having schizophrenia, described the sudden onset of the voices that he heard for the next thirty-two years:

> The voices arrived on an October night in 1962, when I was fourteen years old. Kill yourself . . . set yourself afire, they said. Only a few moments ago I'd been listening to [music] on the small radio on the night table beside my bed. . . . I stirred, thinking I was having a nightmare, but I wasn't asleep; and the voices—low and insistent, taunting and ridiculing—continued to speak to me from the radio. Hang yourself, they told me. The world will be better off without you. You're no good, no good at all.[6]

who speaketh in thee. . . . These be tokens that there are many angels about thee, to keep thee both day and night so that no devil shall have power over thee, nor evil men to harm thee.[7]

Church officials were deeply troubled by Margery Kempe's talk of visions. Eventually they questioned her to determine whether she was a witch. After a lengthy examination they concluded that she was thoroughly orthodox in her beliefs—she was indeed a faithful follower of the church's teachings. Though her visions persisted, Kempe was set free to live out her days amid her family and neighbors.

Thousands of others whose minds conjured strange voices and images were not so fortunate. In medieval Europe, it was perilous to be different, and the church authorities exacted a cruel price.

THE MARKS OF HERESY

The concepts of "freedom of speech" and "freedom of religion" had no place in medieval Europe. The Catholic Church was deeply suspicious of any form of dissent. It maintained its power by instilling fear of punishment in this world and terror of damnation in the next. Anyone who opposed the church's authority by word or action could be designated a heretic, and heresy was a capital crime.

Because they refused to convert to Christianity, Jewish people in Europe were considered enemies of the church. In the 1300s the church in Austria and parts of present-day Germany launched an all-out assault against Jews, executing thousands for religious heresy. In one six-month period, some 100,000 Jews were put to death.

The assault upon Jews swept across Europe, and widened to take in heretics of other varieties as well. Those who practiced witchcraft were clearly a danger to all good Christians. Witches, who used their demonic powers to do the devil's work on Earth, were enemies of the church, heretics in the highest degree. In 1484 Pope Innocent VIII issued a decree, or Papal Bull, calling upon the church to seek out and eradicate witches throughout Christendom.

Most Christians accepted the existence of witches without question. The only controversy lay in how such persons could be

THE IRISH PRINCESS

Sometime in the seventh century, so the legend goes, an Irish princess fled from her home when her widowed father wanted her to marry him. The princess, Dymphna, escaped to the village of Gheel in present-day Belgium. There her irate father caught up with her and had her beheaded. Dymphna was canonized as a Christian martyr. For centuries sick people, especially the insane, visited her tomb. Legend claimed that many insane people were cured at St. Dymphna's shrine.

By the 1400s pilgrims came to Gheel from all over Europe. Townspeople took in mentally ill visitors and helped them to feel at home. At a time when people with mental illnesses were being tortured and burned in much of Europe, Gheel pioneered a remarkable program based on compassion. In the name of St. Dymphna, mentally ill persons were welcomed and accepted as part of the community.

identified, in order that they be properly punished. This problem was resolved in 1486, when two German monks, Heinrich Kramer and James Sprenger, published a book called *Malleus Maleficarum,* or *The Hammer of Witches.* Written in Latin, which at that time served as a common language for educated people in Europe, the book found readers all over the continent.

Chapter by chapter, the *Malleus Maleficarum* describes witchcraft in exhaustive detail. The book explains how witches can be recognized, and prescribes methods for making a witch confess. At the beginning of the book Kramer and Sprenger make it clear that there can be no disagreement with their ideas: "The belief that there are such beings as witches is so essential a part of the Catholic faith that obstinately to retain an opposite

This hand-colored woodcut titled Arresting A Witch
is by Howard Pyle, famous for his illustrations of pirates.

opinion manifestly savors of heresy."[8] Thus anyone who tried to oppose the witch hunt would himself be suspect.

Kramer and Sprenger contended that women were especially susceptible to the black arts. "All wickedness is but little to the wickedness of a woman," they wrote. "Wherefore St. John Chrysostom says: 'It is not good to marry. What else is woman but a foe to friendship, an inescapable punishment, a necessary evil, a natural temptation, a delectable detriment, an evil of nature, painted with fair colors!'"[9] Women who behaved in strange or unusual ways were probably witches and should be examined by an inquisitor. (Since Christ was a man, the authors claimed, males had a degree of immunity from satanic forces.) Anyone, and especially any woman, who talked wildly, wandered aimlessly, and insisted that she heard strange voices or saw visions was likely to be a witch.

Once a suspected witch was arrested, the inquisitors set about to extract a confession. If at first she denied having consorted with the devil, she would generally change her story under torture.

The *Malleus Maleficarum* served as an instruction book for church officials who were eager to carry out the pope's decree. For the next two hundred years clerics referred to its pages as they arrested, questioned, and executed witches from England to Spain, from France and Germany to the kingdoms of Eastern Europe. Tens of thousands of supposed witches were tortured and put to death during this period, known to historians as the Inquisition. Some were religious dissenters—people who dared to question a tenet of church

LOSE/LOSE

In the beginning of the seventeenth century King James I of England popularized a witch-finding technique based on the notion that a pond or river would recognize a witch and refuse to take her in. The suspect was bound hand and foot and tossed into the water. If she floated, her guilt was certain. If the waters embraced her and she sank to the bottom, her innocence was revealed.

doctrine. Some were the victims of gossip and reprisal, accused of witchcraft by a jealous neighbor and forced under torture to confess. Many were people who today would be regarded as mentally ill. Their hallucinations and delusions seemed to be direct messages from the devil himself. Like Margery Kempe, they believed that the devil was tormenting them, threatening them, and trying to drag them toward the fires of hell.

When European colonists came to North America in the 1600s they brought their belief in witchcraft along with them. Approximately forty supposed witches were burned or hanged in colonial New England. The most notorious witch hunt in the New World occurred in Salem, Massachusetts, in 1692, when hundreds of accused witches were imprisoned and nineteen were put to death. Among them was Sarah Good, a homeless woman who muttered to herself and may have been mentally ill.

THE LIGHT OF REASON

During the sixteenth century Western Europe entered an era known as the Renaissance, or Reawakening. Astronomers discovered that the planets revolved around the Sun, refuting the long-held belief that Earth was the center of the universe. Christopher Columbus, an Italian captain sailing under the flag of Spain, accidentally discovered undreamed-of lands across the Atlantic. The Protestant Reformation, led by a German cleric named Martin Luther, broke the dominance of the Roman Catholic Church. In Germany Johannes Gutenberg invented movable type, making books easily available for the first time in history. More and more people learned to read and write. Art and music flourished. Scholars took renewed interest in the learning of the ancient Greeks. Travelers to the Muslim countries returned with the writings of Avicenna and other Arab and

Persian doctors. The medical writings of Hippocrates, Galen, and others came under fresh scrutiny.

As Europe awoke to new ideas and the church's power faded, staunch voices arose to protest the excesses of the Inquisition. One of the Inquisition's most outspoken critics was a Swiss-born physician with the formidable name Philippe Aureolus Theophrastus Bombastus von Hohenheim (1493–1541). Fortunately history has bequeathed him a more manageable name, Paracelsus. Paracelsus railed against the authority of the church and berated the stupidity of witchburners. He also rejected the ancient medical theories of Hippocrates, Galen, and Avicenna. While he was a medical student he once hurled their books into the fire declaring, "My shoe buckles have more wisdom than those men!"[10] When treating mania Paracelsus had his patients drink a foul-smelling brew whose chief ingredient was oil of camphor. He also thought mania could be cured by washing the fingers in abrasive chemicals that burned away the skin. Horrifying as these treatments sound, Paracelsus had taken a giant step away from medieval thinking. He saw all illness, whether of the mind or the body, as treatable with the proper medicines.

The Dutch-born physician Johann Weyer (1515–1566) was another ardent foe of the Inquisition. His masterwork, *De Praestigiis Daemonum* (*The Devil's Deception*), published in 1564, was a direct attack upon the *Malleus Maleficarum* and a defense of the women it condemned. "Thus these wretched women are constantly dragged out to undergo atrocious torment until they would gladly exchange at any moment this most bitter existence for death," Weyer wrote, "and are willing to confess whatever crimes are suggested to them rather than be thrust back into their hideous dungeon and ever recurring torture."[11]

Finally the Inquisition and its practices fell under criticism from within the church itself. In 1623 a German monk routed church officials in a passionate open letter:

> Why do you search so diligently for sorcerers? I will show you at once where they are! Take the Capuchins, the Jesuits, all the religious orders! Torture them! They will confess! If some deny it, repeat it a few times. They will confess. Should a few still be obstinate, exorcise them, shame them, only keep on torturing! They will give in. If you want more, take the canons, the doctors, the bishops of the Church. They will confess. If you want still more, I will torture you, and then you me. I will confess the crimes you will have confessed, and so we shall all be sorcerers together.[12]

At the height of the Inquisition, such an outcry would have meant almost certain death. But by 1623 the hunt for heretics had lost its driving force. With the gradual collapse of the Inquisition came a shift in thinking about the causes and treatment of madness. More and more the mad were seen as suffering from a form of illness. The mad needed to be protected—and society needed protection from the mad.

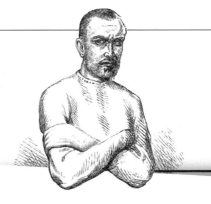

Chapter Four

OUT OF MIND, OUT OF SIGHT

It is to be observed that the basement is appropriated for those patients who are not cleanly in their persons, and who on that account have no beds, but lie on straw with blankets and a rug; but I am sorry to say it is too often made a place of punishment to gratify the unbounded cruelties of the keepers.

— "The Interior of Bethlehem Hospital,"
Urbane Metcalf, 1817

THE SAD, THE BAD, AND THE MAD

When St. Mary of Bethlehem Priory, in London, opened its doors to the sick and destitute in 1329, its nuns acted within the longstanding tradition of Christian charity. At first they took in only a few unfortunates at a time—perhaps a dying leper, or a frail old woman in need of shelter. In 1375 the priory was seized by the Crown, and in 1403 a royal edict turned it into a "mad-house," or shelter for the insane. Records show that the mad-house held six insane men during its first year of operation. The city of London took over the hospital in 1547, and it served as a city hospital for the mentally ill until 1948. By Shakespeare's time the name Bethlehem was shortened to "Bedlam," a word that endures in the English language to this day, connoting unbridled noise and disorder. The word carries an echo of the cacophony that must have reigned in that London institution some five hundred years ago.

LOVING MAD TOM

This traditional song, published in 1720, tells of a mad-woman's search for her lover, Tom, who is confined at Bedlam:

To find my Tom of Bedlam,
Ten thousand years I'll travel.
Mad Maudling goes on dirty toes
To save her shoes from gravel.
Still I sing: bonnie boys! bonnie mad boys!
Bedlam boys are bonnie!
For they all go bare and they live by the air,
And they want no drink nor money.

By the middle of the seventeenth century, public hospitals began to spring up in most of the major cities of Europe. These early institutions were not designed to heal the sick so much as to get them off the streets and prevent them from begging. In former times beggars and madmen had been driven beyond the city gates. Now they were locked away, hidden out of sight. Authorities argued that this confinement was for the good of these poor unfortunates. The laws made it clear, however, that their confinement was also good for the community as a whole.

One of the most famous (and infamous) of these institutions was the Hôpital Géneral, founded in Paris in 1656 by King Louis XIII. An observer wrote that the Salpêtrière, one branch of the Hôpital Géneral, admitted

> pregnant women and girls, wet-nurses and their nurse-lings, male children from seven or eight months to four or five years of age, young girls of all ages, aged married men and women, raving lunatics, imbeciles, epileptics, paralytics, blind persons, cripples, people suffering from ring-worm, incurables of all sorts, children afflicted with scrofula, etc. At the center of this hospital is a house of detention for women comprising four different prisons.[1]

Eventually the Hôpital Géneral held some six thousand people, about 1 percent of the entire population of Paris. One-tenth of those admitted to the Hôpital Géneral were listed as "insane."

Some people were sent to hospitals by the police or a city official. Some, desperate with poverty, applied for admission at the gates. Though the hospitals accepted all comers they offered little to their inmates by way of compassion. To be poor was a disgrace, and to ask for help was shameful. The sick and disabled were marginal members of society, persons of little value.

Frequently their misery was seen as the well-deserved outcome of their own behavior—their laziness, drunkenness, or failure to live a pious life. The hospital provided food and lodging, but it exacted a heavy price in suffering and humiliation.

Each hospital was a kingdom unto itself, with the director as its reigning monarch. The decree founding the Hôpital Géneral appointed the director for life and gave him "all power of authority, of direction, of administration, of commerce, of police, of jurisdiction, of correction and punishment."[2] Furthermore, "the directors having, for these purposes, stakes, irons, prisons, and dungeons in the said Hôpital Géneral, . . . no appeal will be accepted from the regulations they establish within the said hospital."[3] Thus the edict of 1656 gave the directors of the Hôpital Géneral absolute power within the walls of the institution—power over thousands of men, women, and children whom the world outside deemed worthless and undeserving.

Not surprisingly, appalling abuse was rampant. A visitor to the Hôpital Géneral wrote that "the unfortunate whose entire furniture consists of a straw pallet, lying with his head, feet, and body pressed against the wall, could not enjoy sleep without being soaked by the water which trickled from that massive stone."[4] Conditions grew still more ghastly during the winter:

> When the waters of the Seine rose, those cells situated at
> the level of the sewers became not only more unhealthy,
> but worse still, a refuge for a huge swarm of rats which dur-
> ing the night attacked the unfortunates confined there and
> bit them wherever they could reach them. Madwomen have
> been found with feet, hands, and faces torn by bites, which
> are often dangerous, and from which several have died.[5]

The horrors of the Hôpital Géneral were mirrored in other institutions throughout Europe. At Bedlam women were chained by their ankles along the wall of a long gallery. At

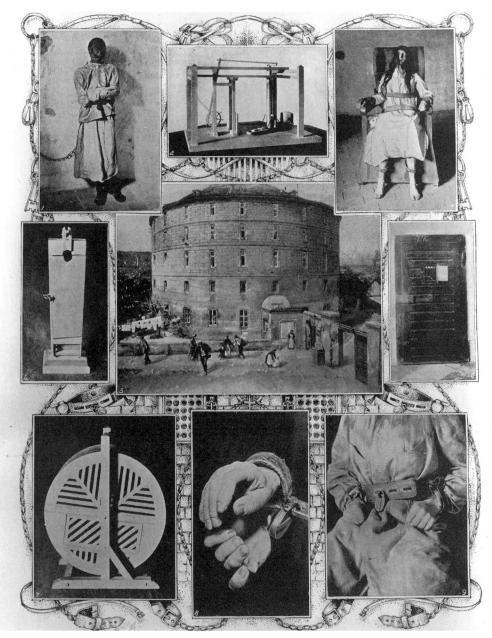

This page from the Illustrated London News *of 1909 is subtitled "How It Was Usual To Treat The Insane in Olden Times." The devices shown are typical of those used all over Europe in the 1800s—devices that would seem capable of driving even the most mentally stable person insane.*

A PENNY A PEEK

During the eighteenth and early nineteenth centuries, enterprising madhouse directors brought in extra funds by putting their charges on display. With mingled horror and fascination people flocked to the institutions where they gawked and jeered at the half-naked inmates, who shrieked, howled, sang, and tore at their hair and bodies. In 1815, testimony before the British House of Commons revealed that curious visitors were admitted to view the lunatics at Bedlam for a penny each Sunday. In one year Bedlam collected four hundred pounds in pennies from some 96,000 visitors.

another English hospital a woman who had epileptic seizures was kept in a pigsty, her hands and feet bound. In Strassburg, France, half-naked men were locked in cages with iron grating beneath their feet.

To the hospital directors, the "keepers" who enforced their commands, and the general public, the inmates of these institutions were not fully human. The rational mind was the essence of humanity, and these howling lunatics had lost their reason. Essentially, mad persons were animals, and could be caged, chained, and even fed like livestock. An eyewitness at one hospital wrote that the inmates were kept in locked cells where

tiny openings pierced next to the doors were fitted with iron bars and shutters. Quite close to this opening hung a chain fastened to the wall and bearing at its end a castiron receptacle, somewhat resembling a wooden shoe, in which food was placed and passed through the bars of these openings.[6]

For the most part, public hospitals made little attempt to provide treatment to their mad inmates. Families with financial means wanted more for their disturbed relatives, and clung to the hope that they could be helped. Late in the seventeenth century a few individuals (only some of whom were doctors) converted crumbling manor houses into small private hospitals. For a substantial fee they offered a variety of treatments for the insane. The directors ran these hospitals as business ventures, and made some extravagant claims. An advertisement in a London newspaper reads:

> In Clerkendale Close . . . there is one who, by the blessing of God, cures all lunatic, distracted, or mad people. He seldom exceeds more than three months in the cure of the maddest person that comes in his house. Several have been cured in a fortnight, and some in less time. He has cured several from Bedlam and other madhouses in and about the city.

The notice concludes with the brash promise, "No cure, no money."[7]

While public officials were busy confining mad persons in grim institutions, physicians continued in their efforts to understand and cure madness in all its forms. Drawing from the writings of predecessors such as Galen, Avicenna, Paracelsus, and Weyer, they sought to unravel the mysteries of the troubled mind.

TAMING THE PASSIONS

"The passions necessarily cause certain movements in the humors," wrote two French physicians in 1682. "Anger agitates the [yellow] bile; sadness excites melancholy, black bile; and the movements of the humors are on occasion so violent that they disrupt the entire economy of the body, even causing death."[8]

ALIENS AND ALIENISTS

The Swiss anatomist Felix Plater (1536–1614) spent years studying mad persons, many of whom he found imprisoned in dungeons as suspected witches. Plater concluded that most emotional disturbance was caused by abnormalities in the brain. He wrote that mad persons suffered from "alienation," that is, their illness separated them from their true selves. At the time few physicians heeded Plater's ideas, but his term "alienation" stuck. Until the late nineteenth century, a doctor who specialized in the treatment of the mentally ill was known as an alienist.

More than two thousand years after Hippocrates proposed his theory of the humors, the notion of these four vital substances was still alive and well in Western Europe. The humors affected emotions and emotions affected the humors. Somehow the action of humors and emotions could send a man or woman hurtling to the depths of madness.

Though physicians actively sought more scientific explanations for mental illness, most found it difficult to break away from the time-honored humoral theory. Due to an excess of black bile, physicians believed, the brain of the melancholic was heavy, wet, and cold. If a person entered a manic state, his brain was overly hot and dry. One popular treatment for mania was cold water, which was thought to cool the overheated brain. The patient was strapped into a chair beneath a device that emptied a pool of ice water through a pipe directly onto his head. The same treatment was prescribed for people with melancholia. Doctors recognized that mania and melancholia were somehow related, since some patients alternated between one extreme state and the other.

Other treatments tried to expel excessive humors from the patient's body. Purges and emetics—drugs that caused diarrhea or vomiting—were thought to cleanse the body of humors that caused disease. Another medical practice was bleeding, in which doctors applied bloodsucking leeches to the patient's arms and legs. These methods were used widely throughout Europe and the American colonies to treat both physical and mental illnesses.

In 1621 an English scholar named Robert Burton published a remarkable 600-page volume called *Anatomy of Melancholy*. Burton was not a physician. He was dean of divinity at England's renowned Oxford University. In writing about melancholia, he drew largely upon his own experience with the condition. He described himself as "an Oxford scholar of great eminence and a recluse who perpetually dreamed of being able to participate in life." When writing about melancholia, he explained the interplay of humors and emotions:

> For anger stirs choler, heats the blood and vital spirits; sorrow on the other side refrigerates the body . . . overthrows appetite, hinders digestion, and perverts the understanding.

MADDENED BY THE MOON

Since ancient times, people have believed that bouts of madness are triggered by the phases of the Moon. The term "lunacy," from the same root as the word "lunar," reflects this belief. Lord Justice Matthew Hale (1606–1676) wrote that the Moon had a powerful influence on human emotions. His writing strengthened the notion that the full Moon sparked or heightened insanity. To this day, police officers and hospital workers sometimes claim that there are more violent crimes and psychiatric admissions on nights of the full Moon.

EXPLORING THE DEPTHS

Many writers since Burton have tried to convey depression's hopelessness and powerlessness. Journalist Tracy Thompson says:

> "My body aches intermittently, in waves, as if I had malaria. I eat with no appetite, . . . I am tired, so tired. . . . At work today I am forgetful; I have trouble forming sentences, I lose track of them halfway through, and my words keep getting tangled. Things seem sad to me. . . . I feel as if my brain were a lump of protoplasm with tiny circuits embedded in it, and some of the wires keep shorting out.[9]

Fear dissolves the spirits . . . attenuates the soul: and for these causes all passions and perturbations must to the uttermost of our power, and most seriously be removed.[10]

Burton's recommendations for the treatment of melancholia sound refreshingly positive to modern ears. Instead of ice-cold showers he suggested a healthful diet, plenty of sleep, soothing music, exercise, and meaningful work. In addition, Burton urged the melancholic to unburden himself to a close friend. "Our best way for ease is to impart our misery to some friend, not to smother it up in our own breast, otherwise the defect increases through concealing it."[11]

Other voices of reason took up the call. They encouraged melancholic patients to go for walks, to take long rides on horseback, and, whenever possible, to enjoy an ocean voyage. The motion and the change of scene were thought to have beneficial effects, easing the mind and restoring a sense of hope.

Eventually the "walking cure" was perverted into a technique Burton could never have imagined or approved. In the

*This 1818 cartoon indicates that some people
questioned the effectiveness of Cox's swing.*

early nineteenth century an English physician, Nathan Cox,
invented a "rotatory machine" for the treatment of manic and
melancholic patients. The patient was strapped to a bed or chair
which swung around a vertical pillar by means of a rotating
beam. The spinning could be speeded up, slowed down, or
stopped abruptly, at the doctor's whim. Not surprisingly, Cox

reported that prolonged spinning at high speed caused the patient to become disturbed and agitated. But if the rotation was carefully controlled, he claimed, the melancholia was driven out. Cox's machine was installed in several hospitals, where it was soon used as a threat to keep difficult patients under control.

For the most part, physicians of the seventeenth and eighteenth centuries recognized two forms of mental disturbance, mania and melancholia. However, a few began to identify other illnesses as well. Thomas Willis (1621–1675) described a condition that medical historians suspect may have been schizophrenia:

> These persons, who were once upon a time clever and gifted, gradually become, without any great changes in their way of life, duller and indeed, foolish or insipid . . . rather as it is with certain wines that after fermentation is completed, lose their strength and little by little turn vapid. A good number, having been to a high degree intelligent during childhood, and extremely quick to learn, end up in adolescence enfeebled and dull. Where they were handsome in aspect before, they are now without gracefulness or pleasant demeanor.[12]

Richard Morton (1637–1698) gives a vivid account of an eighteen-year-old girl with a condition we call anorexia nervosa today. She refused to eat until she looked like "a skeleton clad with skin," and studied tirelessly into the night. Morton treated her by applying plasters to her stomach to draw out the bad humors. He forced her to inhale ammonia fumes to subdue her violent passions, and tried to build up her strength with medicines containing iron. Within a few months the girl died.

As European doctors learned more about the brain by dissecting cadavers, they gradually relinquished the concept of the four humors. Instead, they ascribed many emotional disturbances to problems of the nervous system. Women especially were considered prone to "nervous complaints." Nervous vapors were thought to arise from the uterus, deranging the female brain. Despite their study of anatomy, some physicians returned to an ancient Greek notion that the womb wandered throughout the body in search of children, causing a form of emotional distress called hysteria. Women of the privileged classes were warned to avoid study or hard work which might overtax their delicate nervous systems. Their fathers and husbands tried to protect them from excitement that could bring on an attack of "the vapors."

A wealthy woman who had uncontrolled bouts of tears or who slipped into melancholic withdrawal could consult with a learned physician, while her poverty-stricken counterpart could be turned out into the street. A woman with a nervous disorder might be advised to visit a spa such as Bath in England or Wiesbaden in Germany. Spas grew up around natural mineral springs which were thought to have healing qualities. Women and men with a variety of physical illnesses or nervous complaints visited the spas for weeks or months at a time, bathing in the waters and enjoying a lively social life.

Naturally, the poor did not enjoy the luxury of visits to spas. Nervous complaints were the province of the upper classes. Emotional instability among the poor was far more often regarded as madness. In the late 1700s doctors took a fresh view of treating the mad. For the first time they tried to turn the hospitals of old into places where mad persons might be cured and returned to society.

THE MAD UNCHAINED

In 1793 an idealistic alienist named Philippe Pinel (1745–1826) was appointed director of the Bicêtre, Paris's notorious madhouse for men. France was shuddering with the aftershocks of the bloody upheaval known as the French Revolution. The royal family had been overthrown, and Queen Marie Antoinette had lost her head to the guillotine. The revolution promised a new era of equality, liberty, and brotherhood. The new order would empower the common people and enable them to reach their fullest potential.

When he arrived at Bicêtre, Pinel found many of the patients locked in filthy cells or chained to the walls. He was eager to make changes, to put the ideals of the revolution into action. If he treated these outcasts humanely, surely he could bring forth their inborn humanity. During his first weeks on the grounds Pinel was deeply impressed by Madame Poussin, the wife of one of the hospital officials. "I was astonished at Bicêtre to see her approach the most furious maniacs to calm them with words of consolation," he wrote in his memoir,

> and to get them to eat meals that they would obstinately have rejected from any other hand. One day an insane patient, reduced to danger of starvation from his stubborn refusal to eat, revolted against her, and, pushing away the food she was serving him, reviled her in the most outrageous terms. This quick-witted woman put herself in unison with his delusional notions. She jumped and danced about in front of him, talked back to him in kind, and succeeded in making him smile. Taking advantage of this opportunity to get him to eat, she saved his life.[13]

Madame Poussin's success confirmed Pinel's notion that even the most disturbed patients could benefit from kind and imaginative treatment. He resolved to unchain the madmen of Bicêtre. According to one account, written in 1836, many Parisians were alarmed by Pinel's plan. One local philanthropist asked Pinel for a tour of the institution.

The story of Pinel and his liberation at Bicêtre is a legend in the history of mental health. Contemporary and subsequent accounts were illustrated with varying degrees of drama, this image appearing in Harper's *magazine in 1899.*

Pinel immediately led him to the section for the deranged, where the sight of the cells made a painful impression on him. He asked to interrogate all of the patients. From most he received only insults and obscene apostrophes. It was useless to prolong the interview. Turning to Pinel [he said],

"Now, citizen, are you mad yourself to seek to unchain such beasts?" Pinel replied calmly, "Citizen, I am convinced that these madmen are so intractable only because they have been deprived of air and liberty." "Well, do as you like with them, but I fear you may become the victim of your own presumptions."[14]

A few at a time, Pinel began to release the Bicêtre's inmates from their chains. As he predicted, the patients were grateful for their freedom, and did not attack him or other members of the staff.

While Pinel is often regarded as the father of modern psychiatry, he was not the first European doctor to unchain the patients in his madhouse. Pinel was probably aware of the work of several other, less well-known, physicians who went before him. In his memoir he writes of a visit to a hospital in Spain where humane treatment methods were in use:

> From morning on you can see them . . . leaving daily for the various parts of the vast enclosure that belongs to the hospital, sharing . . . the tasks appropriate to the season— cultivating wheat and vegetables, concerned with the harvest, the trellises, with the vintage, with olive-picking; and finding in the evening in their solitary asylum calm and quiet sleep.[15]

Pinel's reform came at a time when European thought was undergoing radical changes. The eighteenth century is often called the Age of Enlightenment, an era deeply influenced by the work of philosophers such as John Locke and Jean-Jacques Rousseau. These thinkers emphasized the essential worth and goodness of each human being. New democratic ideas swept the Continent, shaking society from top to bottom. They unseated monarchs, created a system of public education, and triggered reforms in prisons and madhouses.

Decades before Pinel unchained his first patient, voices rose in protest of the horrors of the madhouse system. Daniel Defoe, best known as the author of *Robinson Crusoe*, raised public concern that sane people were being locked into madhouses by vindictive relatives. In 1728 he wrote an outraged exposé about husbands

> sending their wives to madhouses at every whim and dislike, that they may be more secure and undisturbed in their debaucheries. . . . This is the height of barbarity and injustice in a Christian country. It is a clandestine inquisition, nay, worse! . . . If they are not mad when they go into these cursed houses, they are soon made so by the barbarous usage they there suffer. . . . Is it not enough to make anyone mad, to be suddenly clapped up, stripped, whipped, ill-fed, and worse use? To have no reason assigned for such treatment, no crime alleged or accusers to confront, and what is worse, no soul to appeal to but merciless creatures who answer but in laughter, surliness, contradictions, and, too often, stripes [lashes with the whip]?[16]

After a series of similar protests, the British Parliament finally investigated private madhouses in London and found that sane people were indeed being incarcerated against their will. In 1774 Parliament passed a law requiring a medical certificate before any non-pauper could be locked away as insane. The law did not cover paupers, and medical certificates were all too easy to come by, even for persons of means.

Other protesters raised public awareness of the cruel treatment of the mad themselves. In 1774 an English wool merchant, Alexander Bruckshaw, published a pamphlet describing his months at a private madhouse in Yorkshire:

> When Wilson [the keeper] showed me to bed he carried me up into a dark and dirty garret, there stripped me and carried my clothes out of the room, which I saw no more

MADNESS ON THE THRONE

In 1788 rumors leaked to the British public that their king, George III, had gone mad. During his long reign George III had several bouts of mental illness, during which he became agitated, irritable, and incoherent. He also suffered an assortment of physical symptoms, including abdominal cramps, swelling of the feet, and coma. The king's royal status did not protect him from the horrors of eighteenth-century treatment. According to one eyewitness, the Countess Harcourt, "The unhappy patient . . . was no longer treated as a human being. His body was immediately encased in a machine which left it no liberty of motion. He was sometimes chained to a stake. He was frequently beaten and starved, and at best he was kept in subjection by menacing and violent language."[17] In addition he was purged, bled, and given emetic drugs. Some medical historians believe that George III had a physical disorder known as porphyria, which can cause severe psychiatric symptoms. The king's madness helped stir Parliament's interest in the treatment of the mentally ill.

for upwards of a month, but lay chained to this bad bed all that time. . . . At the expiration of about a month I was permitted to have my clothes for a day, and to walk about the house in irons.[18]

Early in the 1790s a devout Quaker, William Tuke (1732–1822), led an investigation of English madhouses and was appalled by the conditions he found. At the York Hospital, where a fellow Quaker had recently died under suspicious circumstances, Tuke discovered a tiny room, eight feet square (six square meters), where thirteen women slept on filthy straw. By day they were confined to a room scarcely larger.

Like Pinel, Tuke was convinced that mad persons should be treated with kindness rather than cruelty. He determined to create "a place in which the unhappy might obtain refuge—a quiet haven in which the shattered bark may find a means of reparation or safety."[19] Tuke's institution, the York Retreat, opened its doors in 1796. It heralded a new era in the treatment of the mentally ill, the age of the asylum.

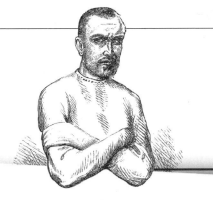

Chapter Five

THE PROMISE OF THE ASYLUM

The inmates . . . all are busy, and delighted by being so. . . . You meet the gardener, the common agriculturalist, the mower, the weeder. . . . The bakehouse, the laundry, the kitchen, are all well supplied with indefatigable workers. . . . There is in this community no compulsion, no chains, no corporal chastisement, simply because these are proved to be less effectual means of carrying any point than persuasion, emulation, and the desire of obtaining gratification. . . . You will pass those who are fond of reading, drawing, music, scattered through handsome suites of rooms, furnished chastely but beautifully. . . . In short, all are so busy as to overlook, or are all so contented as to forget, their misery. Such is a faithful picture of what may be seen in many institutions, and of what might be seen in all, were asylums conducted as they ought to be.

—William A. F. Browne, superintendent of the
Montrose Asylum in Edinburgh, Scotland.

REFORMS AND REALITIES

Dorothea Dix, a Boston schoolteacher, visited England in 1836 at a low point in her life. For more than two years she had battled physical illness and a depressed state of mind. In England she found herself friendless and alone at a dreary Liverpool inn, staring through the window at the endless rain. Her life had no purpose. Her future seemed empty. She did not know how she could go on living.

Fortunately Dorothea Dix (1802–1887) carried a letter of introduction to William Rathbone III, the friend of a Boston acquaintance. The Rathbones took Dix into their home and cared for her with heartfelt warmth. Their kindness broke through her melancholy and restored her interest in life. Within months she was enjoying the lively Rathbone household, where friends streamed in and out and passionate discussions challenged her keen intellect.

Among the many visitors to the Rathbone home was Samuel Tuke, the grandson of William Tuke. Following in his grandfather's footsteps, Samuel was now superintendent of the York Retreat. Dix listened, enthralled, as Tuke described his work with the patients under his care. The retreat occupied a lovely Georgian mansion about a mile from the city. It was surrounded by flower and vegetable gardens, which the patients themselves tended. Tuke ran his program according to the Quaker principles of nonviolence and respect for the individual. He did not restrain his patients with chains or spin them in rotatory machines. Instead he appealed to their innate desire to behave well and regain their powers of reason. Tuke referred to his nonmedical methods as "moral treatment."

In the first decades of the nineteenth century, moral treatment blossomed in institutions all over Europe. Pinel, Tuke, and others wrote eloquently of curing madmen and women who were once considered beyond help. Not only were his patients cured, Pinel insisted, but they became superior beings in the wake of his treatment. "Nowhere except in novels," he boasted, "have I seen spouses more worthy of being cherished, parents more tender, lovers more passionate, or persons more attached to their duties than the majority of the insane, fortunately brought to the period of their convalescence."[1] A German physician, Johan Reil (1759–1813) went so far as to proclaim that madness would soon be eradicated altogether: "The horrors of the prisons and the gaols are over. . . . A bold race of men dares to take on this gigantic idea, an idea that dizzies the normal burgher, of wiping from the face of the earth one of the most devastating of pestilences."[2]

Moral treatment was a radical departure from the medically based treatments of the seventeenth and eighteenth centuries. Most proponents of moral treatment believed that madness was partially the result of biological disease in the body or brain. But they also saw it as a process in the mind, a set of behaviors shaped

NOT GUILTY, ON THE GROUNDS OF INSANITY

In 1843 a Glasgow carpenter named Daniel McNaughton attempted to assassinate British Home Secretary Sir Robert Peel, and accidentally killed Peel's assistant instead. In the celebrated court case that followed, McNaughton's lawyers proved that he had delusions of persecution. For months he had been tormented by the idea that public officials were pursuing him. McNaughton was acquitted of murder on the grounds that he was insane and could not distinguish between right and wrong. The McNaughton case is the foundation of the "insanity plea" that is sometimes invoked in courtrooms to this day.

by the patient's circumstances. According to Pinel, the Tukes, and others, only moral treatment could bring about a cure, and this treatment must be conducted in a "lunatic asylum."

The word "asylum" describes a place of safety and refuge. Bicêtre, the York Retreat, and the many "lunatic asylums" modeled upon them were seen as safe harbors for the insane, places where they would be sheltered from the damaging influences of the outside world. Isolated from the stress of family life, cared for by wise, gentle doctors and attendants, they could learn effective ways to deal with others and unlearn troublesome forms of behavior. The concept of asylum treatment was diametrically opposed to the philosophy behind the earlier madhouses. While the madhouses were largely intended to protect society from its lunatics, the asylums sought to protect lunatics from society.

Work was a key ingredient to moral treatment. According to Tuke, "those kinds of employments are doubtless to be preferred . . . which are accompanied by considerable bodily action, that are most agreeable to the patient, and that are most opposite to the illusions of the disease."[3] Patients at most asylums followed a strict daily routine. At one German institution the patients rose at 5:00 A.M., bathed, and ate breakfast.

TIME FOR TEA

As a special reward, the "best" patients at the York Retreat were invited to tea parties where they mingled with the staff. Such gatherings helped the patients hone their social skills before they returned home. "The guests dress in their best clothes," Samuel Tuke wrote, "and vie with each other in politeness and propriety. . . . The evening generally passes with the greatest harmony and enjoyment. It rarely happens that any unpleasant circumstance occurs."[4]

Between six and seven they listened to readings from the Bible. Throughout the day times were allotted for chores, military exercises, art classes, geography lessons, and finally, "bowling for small prizes."[5]

In retrospect, other facets of moral treatment seem far less benign. The French historian and philosopher Michel Foucault points out that moral treatment replaced physical restraint with other forms of coercion—fear and shame. "The principle of fear," Tuke wrote, "which is rarely decreased by insanity, is considered as of great importance in the management of patients."[6] If a patient raged and kicked the furniture, his attendants reminded him that he would be chained up unless his behavior improved. Pain and terror were also used to jolt unresponsive patients back to life. Johann Reil would drip molten wax upon the patient's skin, or place live mice trapped beneath an inverted glass on her body.

Harsh as those these treatments appear to us today, the physicians who carried them out were convinced that they acted for the patient's good. Like many of his predecessors, Philippe Pinel recommended the use of cold showers to keep patients in line: "Remind him of the transgression or of the omission of an important duty, and with the aid of a faucet suddenly release a shower of cold water upon his head. . . . The madman is made to understand that it is for his sake, and reluctantly, that we resort to such violent measures."[7] Pinel reports the case of a young woman who broke things and tore at her clothes. He scolded her severely and placed her in a straitjacket. She wept for two hours with shame and remorse, and afterward she was docile and meek.

Dorothea Dix knew nothing of the threats and punishments used in European asylums. Her own mental distress had been eased in the loving atmosphere of the Rathbone home. When she returned to the United States, she dreamed of bringing such relief to others.

THE STRAITJACKET IN FRONT.

society," to quote again the words of Dr. Parigot, "the insane may be temporarily deprived of their liberty, it is but a preventive measure, just and acceptable in certain conditions, out of which a positive right must be acknowledged—namely, that the law which forcibly isolates or secludes a patient from his friends and family assumes *pro facto* the responsibility of a real and scientific medical treatment. A public convenience or a public right can never include the violation of an individual one, or the non-accomplishment of a duty."

The greater medical supervision is all the more necessary, in order to turn to account the lucid intervals, and prolong them as far as science can effect it. Now, too

BELT AND SHACKLES USED IN SOME ASYLUMS.

frequently when the lucid interval arrives, the patient is subjected to the same treatment as when reason no longer ruled. Yet in many cases almost complete freedom can

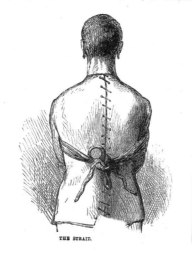

THE STRAIT.

DARK ROOM FOR INSANE PATIENTS.

Philippe Pinel may have unchained the patients at Bicêtre, but many he kept restrained with a garment he called a camisole. We know this garment as a straitjacket. The extra-long sleeves are tied in the back keeping the arms crossed and close to the body. Confinement in a straitjacket can cause agonizing cramps in the arms and hands.

ACROSS THE ATLANTIC

Back in Boston, Dorothea Dix launched an exhaustive investigation of the plight of the mentally ill. She found that most were relegated to prisons, almshouses, and private madhouses. Like the Hôpital Géneral in seventeenth-century Paris, nineteenth-century almshouses were catchall institutions for the unwanted. They sheltered people who were homeless due to poverty, and took in those who were blind, crippled, retarded, mentally ill, or elderly—anyone without the support of family and friends.

During her visits to Massachusetts institutions Dix made detailed notes on everything she saw. In 1842 she presented her findings to the Massachusetts legislature in a pamphlet entitled "Memorial." Eloquently, passionately, Dix described the horrors she had witnessed. At an almshouse in the town of Saugus she discovered

> an apartment entirely unfurnished; no chair, table, nor
> bed; neither a bundle of straw or lock of hay; cold, very
> cold. . . . On the floor sat a woman, her limbs immovably
> contracted, so that the knees were brought upward to the
> chin; the face was concealed; the head rested on the folded
> arms; for clothing she appeared to have been furnished
> with fragments from many discharged garments; these
> were folded about her, yet they little benefited her, if one
> might judge by the constant shuddering which almost con-
> vulsed her poor crippled frame.[8]

At the Newburyport almshouse, in a closet beneath the cellar stairs, she found "a female apparently wasted to a skeleton, partially wrapped in blankets, [her face withered] not by age, but by suffering." When the woman saw Dix and the almshouse keeper, she stretched out her arms and cried, "Why am I consigned to hell? Dark—dark! I used to pray—I used to read the

Bible—I have done no crime in my heart; I had friends—why have all forsaken me? My God! My God! Why hast thou forsaken me?"[9]

How could Christians permit such cruelty and degradation in their communities, Dix demanded to know. Under humane conditions, the women and men she described could find comfort and peace. Perhaps their reason might even be restored. Such humane treatment, she believed, could be provided in asylums, or mental hospitals, designed specifically for the care and treatment of the insane.

After Dix presented the "Memorial," the Massachusetts legislature voted to expand the state-run mental hospital at Worcester, and to transfer there the insane who were held in jails and almshouses around the state. Buoyed by her success, Dix traveled from state to state, investigating, reporting, and urging legislatures to create asylums for their insane citizens. Her success was remarkable. In some instances, previously existing hospitals were enlarged. At other times she persuaded lawmakers to found new facilities. Idealistic asylum superintendents studied moral treatment methods and tried their best to put them into practice.

Many patients flourished under the gentle handling at these small early asylums, which seldom held more than fifty or a hundred patients at a time. In the homelike atmosphere, where the superintendent served as a firm but benevolent father figure, patients put aside their fears and agitation and settled into a comfortable routine. Some patients wrote moving letters of gratitude after they were discharged. "When I sometimes tremble for the future," wrote one woman to the superintendent of the Pennsylvania Hospital in Philadelphia, "there arises a strong feeling of confidence in looking toward you." Another explained, "I now see clearly that it was a disease that led me to pursue the course of conduct I did. . . . Owing to your constant

SEPARATE AND UNEQUAL

Native-born white Americans sometimes argued that immigrants and African Americans had a special tendency toward mental illness. In the years before the Civil War, several "scientific" studies supposedly proved that free blacks had a higher rate of physical and mental illness than did slaves. Thus blacks must be unfit to cope with freedom, and were better off under slavery. In 1851 one doctor, Samuel Cartwright, detailed two mental diseases he claimed were unique to blacks: drapetomania and dysaesthesia Aethiopis. Cartwright described drapetomania as a condition that caused slaves to run away. It was common, he wrote, among slaves "whose masters made themselves too familiar with them, treating them as equals."[10] Dysaesthesia Aethiopis resulted in a desire to avoid work and cause mischief—overseers referred to it as "rascality." Many physicians immediately recognized that these diagnoses were merely a means to justify the enslavement of African Americans.

Asylum directors stated that it was their duty to serve all patients, regardless of race or ethnic background. But segregation in U.S. asylums began as early as the 1840s. Some hospitals in Northern cities opened separate wards for immigrants from Ireland, lest they offend the sensibilities of native-born American patients. African Americans were usually treated in separate wings or, in the Southern states, in entirely separate hospitals. Some states, including Ohio and Indiana, had no facilities for black patients, and denied them treatment altogether.

and unvarying kindness I was first led seriously to reflect, to reason with myself about it."[11]

A patient was discharged when she or he could function adequately on the outside. Some institutions claimed that as many as 50 percent of their patients left within a year of admission, never to return. Between 1843 and 1845 the Worcester State Hospital in Massachusetts claimed a cure rate of 82 to 90 percent. What these statistics really mean, in modern terms, remains cloudy.

The period of optimism was short-lived. As the years passed, the state asylums could not keep up with the number of patients in need of treatment. State legislatures balked at rising costs. Poorly trained attendants, with little grasp of the goals of moral treatment, struggled to maintain order on chaotic, overcrowded asylum wards. In 1851 one superintendent told Dorothea Dix, "The tendency now is not to make hospitals as fit as possible, but as cheap as possible."[12]

THE COLLAPSE OF THE DREAM

"I cannot know the daily changes in the symptoms of 450 patients," lamented the superintendent of a Massachusetts asylum in 1848. "If [the superintendent] has under his charge more than one hundred, it is difficult to know their personal history and the daily changes in their condition."[13] The population of the United States mushroomed in the second half of the nineteenth century, and so did the number of people needing treatment in asylums. According to census figures, in 1840 the U.S. population was 17 million, of whom approximately 17,000 were insane or "feebleminded." (Early census figures did not differentiate between mental illness and mental retardation.) Of those 17,000, some 2,500 were living in asylums, almshouses, or prisons.

Fifty years later, in 1890, the U.S. population had nearly quadrupled to reach 63 million, of whom 106,000 were considered insane. About 74,000 of these mentally ill persons were housed in asylums and other institutions. Thus, in 1840, about

1 person in every 1,000 was counted to be insane or mentally retarded. By 1890 nearly 1 person in 500 was regarded as insane. Almost three quarters of these insane persons were living in institutions. (Even after the asylum movement was well under way, thousands of mentally ill persons continued to be held in almshouses and prisons.)

The champions of moral treatment envisioned institutions that were small and homelike. But most state legislators felt it was cheaper to build a few large asylums instead

THE UTICA CRIB

In 1846 the Utica Asylum in upstate New York pioneered the use of a criblike bed with a locked lid to restrain patients at night. The Utica crib, as the device came to be known, was soon common in hospitals throughout the country. Hospitals claimed that the crib helped an agitated patient to rest by restricting him to his bed. However, many patients became even more frenzied as they pounded on the lid, fighting to escape.

of many small, intimate ones. By the 1880s many state asylums (eventually called state hospitals) held a thousand patients or more. Patients seldom saw their doctors. The ward attendants, who were with the patients all day, had little idea how to treat their illnesses. They spent their time trying to maintain order, struggling to keep the patients under control.

In nineteenth-century England, most hospitals abandoned the use of straitjackets and other mechanical restraints. Following the precepts of moral treatment, they encouraged the asylum staff to win the patients' trust. Patients were urged to take responsibility for their actions. Dr. John Conolly, a British advocate of the nonrestraint method, wrote: "Restraints and neglect may be considered synonymous, for restraints are merely a substitute for the thousand attentions required by troublesome patients."[14]

In the United States, however, physical restraint was part of hospital care well into the twentieth century. Asylum directors and legislators argued that it was more cost-effective to use

TRIAL BY HER PEERS

In 1860 an Illinois minister, Theophilus Packard, committed his wife, Elizabeth, to the state asylum at Jacksonville because she refused to accept his religious beliefs. Under an Illinois law, a husband had the right to commit his wife to an asylum simply by claiming that she was insane. After her release three years later, Elizabeth Parsons Ware Packard lobbied the state legislature to change the law. In 1867 Illinois passed a law requiring a trial by jury in order to commit a man or woman to a mental hospital. Several other states followed the example of Illinois. Elizabeth Packard is remembered as one of the first advocates for patients' rights in the United States.

In the final decades of the 1800s, psychiatrists took a pessimistic view of serious mental illness. Gone was the optimistic flush of the moral treatment movement. Now hospital directors sought to manage their charges, rather than provide them with treatment. Mad patients were beyond hope. Madness was incurable.

Meanwhile, in faraway Vienna, a group of doctors took a radical new approach to the human mind. Their ideas revolutionized the field of psychiatry and transformed Western thought about the human mind.

restraints than to hire additional staff. Some even insisted that nonrestraint could not work in the United States, due to the feisty American character. "Our patients, by some inherent quality in the Yankee, will not submit to the control of any person they consider their equal or their inferior as readily as that of mechanical appliances," wrote the director of the Boston Lunatic Asylum in 1874.[15] Some hospitals routinely put patients in restraints on weekends and holidays when few attendants were on duty. What was best for the patient did not matter. All that mattered was what was easiest for the staff.

The horrors of asylum life in the late nineteenth century bear a chilling resemblance to those of Bedlam and the Hôpital Géneral two centuries before. Upon release a few patients wrote powerful descriptions of their experiences in an attempt to heighten public awareness and bring about reform. In 1869 a businessman named Ebenezer Haskell published the story of his months as a patient at the Pennsylvania Hospital for the Insane. Haskell wrote that he and other patients were regularly kicked and beaten by the staff. His narrative reveals a horrific new method of the "cold-water treatments" so popular in eighteenth-century Europe: "A disorderly patient is stripped naked and thrown on his back. Four men take hold of the limbs and stretch them out at right angles. Then the doctor or some one of the attendants stands up on a chair or table and pours a number of buckets full of cold water on his face until life is nearly extinct. Then the patient is removed to his dungeon, cured of all diseases.[16]

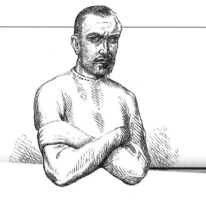

Chapter Six

FROM TRANCE TO TRANSFERENCE

I was a spectator of Bernheim's astonishing experiments upon his hospital patients, and I received the profoundest impression of the possibility that there could be powerful mental processes which nevertheless remained hidden from the consciousness of men.

—Sigmund Freud, 1889

THE POWER OF SUGGESTION

The science of electricity was brand-new in the late 1700s, and Franz Anton Mesmer (1734–1815) found it fascinating. As a young physician practicing in Vienna, Mesmer strove to understand the physical principles that governed electricity and magnetism. A man of forceful imagination, he conceived a startling new theory to explain human illnesses. An invisible fluid, which he called "animal magnetism," fell to earth from the stars. Like electricity, this mysterious fluid had positive and negative charges. The magnetic fluid existed in all living things, and flowed from one to another. In healthy people and animals the negative and positive charges were in equilibrium. If the charges became unbalanced, disease was the result. Mesmer's theory of animal magnetism is reminiscent of the earlier theory of humors, which had been abandoned by most doctors and scientists by Mesmer's time. Like the magnetic fluid, the four humors caused disease when they were out of balance. And like the doctors of the Renaissance, Mesmer sought to restore a crucial equilibrium within his patients.

To bring the charges into balance Mesmer sat with his patient knee to knee. He held the patient by the thumbs and stared into her eyes. Then he passed his hands up and down her arms and legs, seeking to rebalance the magnetic fluid in her body. He repeated this process during several healing sessions, each lasting about an hour. After a number of such sessions, some of Mesmer's patients burst into strange fits of laughter, tears, or shaking. After this "hysterical crisis," as Mesmer called it, the patient's symptoms disappeared.

In 1778 Viennese authorities accused Mesmer of touching his female patients inappropriately, and drove him out of the city. Undaunted, Mesmer settled in Paris, where he won an

SPECIAL EFFECTS

In Paris Mesmer developed a "magnetizing machine," which he called the *baquet*. The baquet consisted of a round oak tub filled with magnetized iron filings. Patients sat around the tub and grasped steel rods that protruded from its lid. Wearing a long purple robe for added effect, Mesmer waved his hands to stir the invisible fluid that rose from the iron filings. Sometimes he played unexpected, earsplitting notes on the glass harmonica, a musical instrument invented by Benjamin Franklin.

The amazing new technology of electricity encouraged the medical profession to experiment with potentially disastrous results. This is the Electric Bathroom of a Michigan sanitarium in 1900.

Mesmer's "magnetizing machine"

eager following among the French aristocracy. So many people flocked to receive his treatments that he held group sessions.

At last the French king, Louis XVI, ordered a scientific investigation into Mesmer's claims. Among the investigators was the American patriot, philosopher, and scientist Benjamin Franklin, who was in France at the time on a diplomatic mission. In its final report, issued in 1784, the committee thoroughly debunked Mesmer's theory. "There is no proof of [the magnetic fluid's] existence," the report states. "The violent effects observed . . . are to be attributed to the touching, to the aroused imagination, and to that mechanical imitation which leads us, in spite of ourselves, to repeat that which strikes our senses."[1] Ironically, the investigating committee was so busy disposing of the concept of animal magnetism that it failed to recognize Mesmer's true discovery, the extraordinary power of the mind in causing and healing illness.

Despite the committee's report, Mesmer's disciples continued to practice and refine his techniques. In the 1870s Mesmerism captured the interest of Jean-Martin Charcot (1825–1893), the doctor in charge of the insane patients at the Salpêtrière in Paris. Many of Charcot's patients had tremors, paralysis, fainting spells, and other symptoms with no known physical cause. This condition, which was especially common among women in the late nineteenth century, was known as hysteria. Charcot decided to use a form of mesmerism, which he called hypnosis, on some of his hysterical patients. Dispensing with iron filings and magnetized rods, he asked the patient to focus on his voice or to stare at a rhythmically moving object. In this way he put her into a deep trance, during which she was highly receptive to his suggestions. He told her that her symptoms would disappear upon awakening, and often she awoke to find herself cured.

Like Mesmer before him, Charcot won acclaim for his astonishing success. Patients arrived from all over France. A young woman who had been paralyzed for years suddenly rose from her stretcher and walked. A woman with severe tremors was able to sit in complete repose. Patients who had suffered from debilitating weakness grew strong enough to return to their work. In 1872, nearly a century after the report that debunked Mesmer's theories, Charcot presented his theory of hypnosis to the illustrious French Academy of Sciences. He explained that hysterical symptoms such as paralysis resulted from a physical weakness in the nervous system. This weakness made the patient dangerously susceptible to certain harmful ideas. In a hypnotic trance these ideas could be dislodged through the power of suggestion.

The Academy of Science greeted Charcot's presentation with enthusiasm. In the French city of Nancy, several more neurologists experimented with hypnosis. Among the most successful of these was Hipolyte Bernheim (1840–1919). In 1889 Bernheim demonstrated his hypnotic methods to a thirty-three-year-old neurologist who was visiting from Vienna. The demonstration made such a lasting impression upon the visitor that he began to rethink his understanding of the human mind. He went on to become the most famous doctor and theorist the field of mental health has ever produced. His name was Sigmund Freud.

THE MAGIC OF WORDS

As a young physician, Sigmund Freud (1856–1939) chose to specialize in neurology, the study of the brain. Until his first visit to Paris in 1886, he wholeheartedly believed that all mental disorders had physiological roots. But his studies under Charcot, and later his visit to Bernheim at Nancy, flung open the door to a set of radical new ideas. What was happening to the patients he observed, who responded so dramatically under hypnosis? Somehow, in the hypnotic trance, they touched parts of themselves that lay hidden from their ordinary consciousness.

When Freud returned to Vienna he shared his excitement over hypnotism with an older doctor, Josef Breuer (1840–1925). Breuer in turn told Freud about a fascinating hysterical patient he had treated several years before. Together they reviewed Breuer's meticulous records, deepening their understanding of the patient's mysterious illness and cure. In 1895 the case of "Anna O." was the fulcrum of their book *Studies in Hysteria*.

In 1880, at the age of twenty-one, the woman Breuer called Anna O. was nursing her father through his final illness. Breuer was first called in when Anna lost her appetite and seemed on the brink of exhaustion. Over the next two years, she developed an array of bizarre symptoms. At one point she lost the ability to speak or understand her native German, and could communicate only in English. Sometimes she thought her own braids were black snakes coming to choke her. She developed two completely separate personalities—one meek and gentle, the other angry and rebellious. Anna believed that the people around her were merely wax figures. The only person who was real to her was Dr. Breuer, who visited faithfully several times each week.

As her condition worsened, Breuer sensed that something weighed upon Anna's mind. He began to question her about events in her life around the time she fell ill. During their sessions Anna began a process that she called "chimney-sweeping," or a "talking cure." In minute detail she described the horrors of her father's illness and her fear and grief as she awaited his death. "These memories were the psychical events involved in the incubation of her illness," Breuer wrote later. "It was they that had produced the whole of the hysterical phe-

Years after her treatment with Breuer, Anna O., whose real name was Bertha Pappenheim, became a women's rights crusader and also fought for the protection of abandoned children.

nomenon, and when they were brought to verbal utterance, the symptoms disappeared."[2]

After studying Anna O.'s case, Freud tried to help his own patients talk about their troubling memories. He was never a skilled hypnotist, but he discovered that a hypnotic trance was not really necessary. While his patient relaxed, lying on a couch, Freud encouraged him to say whatever came into his mind. As the patient talked, he revealed more and more about himself. This technique, which Freud called "free association," was key to the treatment process Freud developed. This form of treatment, or therapy, is known as psychoanalysis.

In the first decades of the twentieth century Freud's ideas continued to evolve. He concluded that long-repressed childhood memories can trigger symptoms in adulthood. Often these repressed memories had to do with childhood sexual desires and aggressive impulses. Such desires and impulses were forbidden to the child, and were forced down into the unconscious mind. There they lay dormant until stirred by some crisis in later life, when they were converted into hysterical paralysis or some other symptom. When the patient became fully conscious of these painful early experiences he was freed from his symptoms at last. "Once a picture has emerged from the patient's memory, we may hear him say that it becomes fragmentary and obscure in proportion as he proceeds with his description of it," Freud wrote. "The patient is, as it were, getting rid of it by turning it into words."[3]

In 1899 Freud published one of his most important works, *The Interpretation of Dreams*. Dreams were the mind's way of conveying secret messages. Their interpretation, Freud wrote, was "the royal road to a knowledge of the unconscious mind." The imagery of the dream "was no more than a distorted, abbreviated, and misunderstood translation" of an individual's unique mental structure.[4]

As his work progressed, Freud noticed that the patient often formed an intense emotional attachment to the therapist. The therapist became a kind of substitute parent. By re-creating his relationship with his father or mother, this time on a healthier footing, the patient was able to let go of harmful memories and behavior patterns. Freud used the term "transference" to describe this bond between patient and therapist. Transference was an essential component of psychoanalytic treatment.

Freud's ideas seemed revolutionary to the medical establishment of his day. Yet he was pulling together theories and treatment methods that dated back thousands of years. Shamans, priests, and mesmerists all encouraged their "patients" to get rid of disturbing memories. Historical accounts by people with mental illness express the critical importance of talking about painful feelings and experiences. In the fifteenth century Margery Kempe believed that her madness descended when she was unable to make her confession to the parish priest. Robert Burton emphasized that a person with melancholia should speak freely to a trusted friend.

Words carried crucial meaning in the chants of the shamans, the priests of Asklepios, and the exorcists of the Middle Ages. Freud, too, recognized the power of words to bring about healing. "Words are the essential tool of mental treatment," Freud wrote in 1890. "A layman will no doubt find it hard to understand how pathological disorders of the body and mind can be eliminated by words. He will feel that he is being asked to believe in magic. And he will not be so very wrong, for the words which we use in our everyday speech are nothing other than watered-down magic. But we shall have to follow a roundabout path in order to explain how science sets about restoring to words a part at least of their former magical power."[5]

DISCIPLES AND DISSENTERS

To the middle classes of Austria and Germany, psychoanalysis overflowed with promise. By releasing themselves from their long-repressed memories, analytic patients hoped to put aside anxiety and sadness, to stride into a future free from fear. Psychoanalysis appealed strongly to educated, articulate women and men who were functioning relatively well at work and at home, despite some troubling anxieties or nightmares. They had plenty of time and money to spend on the analyst's couch. In the first decades of the twentieth century young alienists opened "nervous clinics" to treat such patients, who have sometimes been referred to as "the worried well."

This photograph of Sigmund Freud reviewing the printed sheets of one of his books was taken in 1938.

THE PLIGHT OF THE TAILORS

When Alfred Adler worked at a free clinic in one of Vienna's poorest neighborhoods, many of his patients were tailors. Adler was horrified by the conditions under which they labored. Most tailors worked 12- to 18-hour days in damp, poorly ventilated, dimly lit shops. They developed a variety of work-related ailments, both physical and emotional. A dedicated social reformer, Adler campaigned for better working conditions for the poor of Vienna, especially those who toiled with needle and thread.

Freud did not envision psychoanalysis as a treatment for people with severe mental illnesses, the men and women who filled the asylums. He felt that the truly insane—uneducated, poor, floundering in their delusions—were largely beyond hope. Freud and his disciples focused their efforts on people they felt could benefit from the talking cure.

Yet some of Freud's most devoted followers began to challenge his core ideas, and to strike out on their own. Alfred Adler (1870–1937) felt that Freud's concern with repressed sexual fantasies was much too narrow. He recognized that many factors within the family and the wider society could damage an individual's sense of worth and fill him with feelings of inferiority. Women, the poor, and the disabled were all made to feel powerless and devalued. All human beings, Adler believed, needed encouragement from others in order to reach their full potential.

Like Adler, Carl Gustav Jung (1875–1961) began his career as a Freudian psychoanalyst. He, too, felt cramped by Freud's view of human yearnings and frustrations. Jung believed that all people, of whatever class and culture, are connected to a "collective unconscious" that has evolved through thousands of years of human experience. He described a host of "archetypal symbols" pertaining to universal human experiences such as birth and death. Jung emphasized the spiritual side of human nature, which he felt was key to healing emotional pain.

Adler and Jung had a major rift with Freud in 1911, and each went on to make his own mark in the rapidly expanding field of psychotherapy. Nevertheless, Freudian analysis and Freudian theories held their ground in Europe until World War II. Despite its limitations, Freud's work deepened and strengthened our understanding of the unconscious mind.

Chapter Seven

BEHIND THE WALLS

In the asylum the patient becomes part of a great iron machine, which continues to revolve, carrying her with it. Very little attention is paid to her in particular; and inquiries in regard to leaving meet with no response.

—Kate Lee, a patient at
Elgin State Hospital
in Illinois, 1899–1900

VOICES OF PROTEST

In 1900 a Connecticut businessman named Clifford W. Beers jumped from a fourth-floor window in an attempt to commit suicide. Miraculously Beers survived the fall, but while he lay in his hospital bed, his mind swirled with delusions of guilt and persecution. Over the next three years, confined in a series of private and public asylums, Beers imagined himself at the center of a web of evil. All of the people around him were detectives, intent on uncovering his crimes. For the first two years Beers remained mute and withdrawn, trusting no one. Then, almost overnight, his illness shifted into a manic phase. He talked incessantly and wrote long letters to friends and public officials. When he ran out of writing paper he cut wrapping paper into four-foot (one-and-a-quarter-meter) strips, and kept on writing his frenzied messages to the world.

During his manic phase Beers determined to write a book about the horrific treatment of patients in psychiatric institutions. When his illness finally receded, he held onto this sense of purpose. In 1908 Beers published an autobiography, entitled *A Mind That Found Itself*. Though Beers acknowledges that he desperately needed hospital care, his book is an eloquent protest against the treatment he and other patients received. Of the first private institution where he was confined, he wrote:

> Outside the limits of a city, . . . the owner of this little settlement of woe had erected a nest of veritable fire-traps in which helpless sick people were forced to risk their lives. This was a necessary procedure if the owner was to grind out an exorbitant income on his investment. . . . Its worst manifestation was the employment of the meanest type of attendants, men willing to work for the paltry wage of eighteen dollars a month.[1]

He describes the torment of his first night in a straitjacket:

Within one hour of the time I was placed in it I was suffering pain as intense as any I ever endured, and before the
night had passed it had become almost unbearable. . . .
Soon knife-like pains began to shoot through my right arm
as far as the shoulder. After four or five hours the excess of
pain rendered me partially insensible to it. But for fifteen
consecutive hours I remained in that instrument of torture,
and not until the twelfth hour, after breakfast-time the next
morning, did an attendant so much as loosen the cords.[2]

Beers's book received the endorsement of several leading
writers and reformers, including the renowned psychologist and
philosopher William James. After the book appeared, Beers traveled throughout the country. He spoke to doctors, state officials,
and philanthropic organizations on behalf of psychiatric
patients and their families. Beers argued that mental disorders
are illnesses just like the diseases that beset the body, and that
mentally ill persons should be treated with compassion.

Clifford Beers was not the first former patient to reveal the
horrors of institutions and call for improved treatment. He followed in the footsteps of Alexander Bruckshaw, Elizabeth Parsons Ware Packard, and many others. But at the dawn of the
twentieth century, the world was more willing to listen than ever
before. Muckraking journalists were exposing the excesses of
corporations and political machines. Dedicated social reformers
worked to improve conditions in factories and to abolish child
labor. Women marched in the streets to gain the right to vote,
and African Americans voiced their anguish over "dreams
deferred." It was a time for reflection and a time for action.
Beers spoke openly about his own experiences and laid out a
series of steps that would make mental hospitals more humane
and effective. People began to listen.

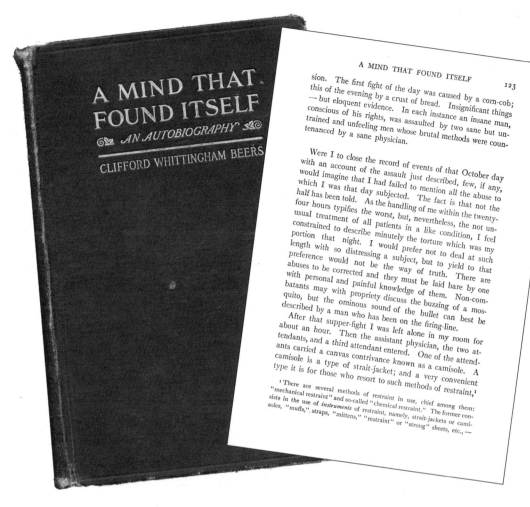

It is easy to understand how readers of the time found Beers's autobiography so compelling. In 1908 people were beginning to demonstrate against sweatshops and child labor. The time was ripe for mental health reform as well.

In 1909 Beers helped to establish the National Committee on Mental Hygiene. The organization sought to educate the public about the nature of mental illness and to push for better treatment in and outside of hospitals. It urged that hospital attendants receive proper training and adequate salaries. The mental-hygiene movement, of which Clifford Beers is consid-

WAYWARD YOUTH

As a teacher in Vienna, August Aichhorn (1878–1949) had remarkable success with some of the most difficult students. Eventually he left teaching and turned his talents to psychotherapy with children and teens. Aichhorn believed that hostile, aggressive adolescents gained nothing from being punished and coerced. Instead he involved them in hiking, sports, art projects, and other activities. In his 1928 book, *Wayward Youth*, Aichhorn notes that disturbed teens usually come from an environment where "the parents lived in an atmosphere of hatred and discord; insults and fighting were parts of their daily life."[3] Aichhorn tried to create an atmosphere where teens could learn more positive values. His work served as a model for programs around the world.

ered the founder, sought to develop community-based programs to prevent mental illness and promote mental health. Mental hygiene was defined as "the promotion of the best development of the individual mind and its mental capacities."[4]

Before the twentieth century, countless physicians and philosophers had promised cures for mental illness. But Freud and his followers opened a new realm of possibility. Their work suggested that mental disorders might actually be prevented from developing in the first place. If mental illness was the result of childhood distress, as Freud claimed, then compassionate child-rearing would go a long way toward creating a healthy, stable populace. Proponents of the mental-hygiene movement lobbied to establish child-guidance clinics in cities across the United States. At these clinics psychiatrists, social workers, and other mental-health professionals provided therapy for troubled children and counseling for their parents. The mental-hygiene movement also encouraged communities to offer children wholesome activities through sports and recreation programs.

Many psychoanalytically oriented therapists put the blame squarely on the shoulders of mothers. Mother emphatically did NOT know best. She was either overprotective or rejecting, demanding or neglectful. No matter what she did, she was seen as a destructive force in her child's life.

The term "refrigerator mom" came to describe a mother who was cold and distant. Refrigerator moms were thought to cause autism, a very severe form of emotional disturbance that begins in early childhood. For generations of mothers, the anguish of witnessing a child's inner turmoil was compounded by feelings of shame and guilt. Somehow, the authorities insisted, the problem was all the mother's fault.

The last decades of the twentieth century saw mounting evidence that severe mental disorders have biological roots. Finally mothers began to shed some of their guilt, to put aside the tormenting question: "What did I do wrong?"

BACK TO THE SNAKE PIT

Between 1931 and 1938, a schoolteacher named Margaret Isabel Wilson was a patient in a private psychiatric hospital near Washington, D.C. "For the new patients, the lesson was taught at once," she wrote later.

> There was no liberty at all for us. We learned to jump up briskly at the sound of the rising bell, and to dress speedily without answering back. . . . We, the more capable ones, would voluntarily make our hasty toilets and were ordered to go directly to the sitting room after the bathroom was locked. We could not go back to get a bit of privacy; it was against the ordinance.[5]

FIGHTING TOOTH DECAY

"Without exception, the functional psychotic patients all have infected teeth," wrote Dr. Henry A. Cotton, appointed superintendent of New Jersey's Trenton State Hospital in 1907. Cotton was convinced that tooth decay was among the leading causes of serious mental illness. Though no scientific evidence supported his claim, he extracted teeth, unchallenged, for nearly three decades. In 1930 a visitor to the hospital wrote, "I felt sad seeing hundreds of people without teeth. . . . They suffer from indigestion, I was told, not being able to masticate the ordinary food which they get."[6]

By the 1930s most hospitals were severely overcrowded and understaffed. They controlled their patients by imposing rigid routines and a strict code of rules. Many patients spent years in these institutions, each day following the last in numbing monotony.

If a patient was willful or rebellious, the staff had ways to make her submit. Hydrotherapy, designed as a form of treatment, was all too frequently used to punish the unruly. Hydrotherapy bore a sinister resemblance to the water treatments of the eighteenth and nineteenth centuries. One woman, Frances Farmer, describes her encounter with hydrotherapy at a public hospital in the state of Washington early in the 1940s. Restrained by a straitjacket, she was lowered into an empty tub and strapped securely into place. Then, as she lay bound and helpless,

> the first crash of icy water hit my ankles and slid rapidly up my legs. I began to shake from the shock of it, screaming and thrashing my body under the sheet, . . . Hydro was

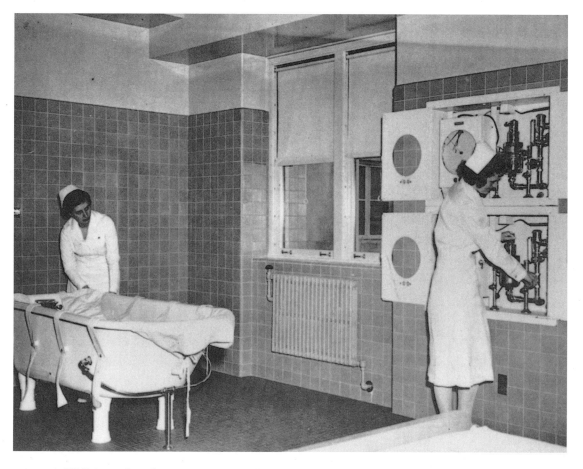

Well-intentioned nurses prepare a bathtub for a patient's hydrotherapy session.

a violent and crushing method of shock treatment, even though it was intended to relax the patient. What it really did was assault the body and horrify the mind until both withered with exhaustion."[7]

Patients were kept in ice water for three hours or more at a time, and might be subjected to these treatments every day for two to three weeks.

Meanwhile, psychiatrists experimented with other methods for treating severe mental illness. Doctors in the United States first used insulin-shock therapy in 1934. The patient received a series of insulin injections, the dosage increasing each day, until his blood sugar plummeted and he lost consciousness. The patient was kept in a coma for about twenty minutes, then revived with a glucose injection to rush sugar back into his bloodstream. Psychiatrists and some patients claimed that insulin shock was dramatically effective in relieving depression. A psychiatrist who pioneered this treatment declared, "The personality of the patient can often be changed so entirely . . . that it seems as though the treatment has created a new being."[8] Nevertheless, many patients were terrified by these treatments, which left them feeling helpless and disoriented. One out of every hundred died in the comatose state. Despite these drawbacks, insulin-shock treatment was widely used until the 1960s.

In the late 1930s an Italian psychiatrist named Ugo Cerletti (1877–1963) examined a group of patients who had epilepsy, a neurological disorder that causes convulsions. He concluded that people with epilepsy did not develop schizophrenia. Cerletti believed that the two conditions were somehow incompatible. If he could produce convulsions in his schizophrenic patients, he reasoned, perhaps their psychotic symptoms would disappear. In 1938 Cerletti experimented on a man found wandering on the streets of Rome, rambling about enemies who controlled him with their thoughts. Cerletti placed wires on the patient's temples and passed an electric current through his brain. The man's body convulsed violently. But after three shocks, Cerletti reported, "The patient sat up, calm and smiling, as though to inquire what we wanted of him."[9] After eleven treatments he was well enough to go home and return to work.

Cerletti's original reasoning was flawed; people with epilepsy can and do develop schizophrenia. However, for reasons that are still not clearly understood, electroconvulsive therapy (ECT) proved to be a major breakthrough. ECT can—at least temporarily—lift the clouds of depression or ease the tortured mind of the schizophrenic. As one doctor wrote, "Without ECT I would not have lasted in psychiatry. I would not have been able to tolerate the sadness and hopelessness of most mental illness before the introduction of convulsive therapy."[10] However, ECT can cause permanent loss of memory. One woman, who had more than one hundred shock treatments over a ten-year period, explains, "I have large, unpredictable blank spots in my life history—unexpected, gaping, empty spaces I cannot fill. . . . ECT caused me excruciating pain, both psychic and physical, but I did emerge intact. I was very lucky."[11]

Egas Moniz, a Portuguese physician, is associated with one of the grimmest episodes in modern mental-health treatment. In 1935 Moniz developed a surgical treatment which, he claimed, could calm highly disturbed patients. The following year, an American psychiatrist named Walter Freeman brought Moniz's technique to the United States. The surgery, known as

THE KENNEDYS' SECRET

As a child Rosemary Kennedy, the sister of President John F. Kennedy, was slow and awkward. She apparently had a form of mild mental retardation. In her late teens Rosemary's personality underwent a catastrophic change. She became angry, rebellious, and physically violent—sometimes shrieking, hitting, and kicking when she did not get her way. Her father, businessman and diplomat Joseph P. Kennedy, consulted with Dr. Walter Freeman in 1941. Freeman recommended a prefrontal lobotomy to bring Rosemary's behavior under control. The surgery left Rosemary with massive brain damage. No longer able to communicate or care for her basic needs, she was placed in a nursing home. The public did not learn the truth about Rosemary's surgery until 1996.

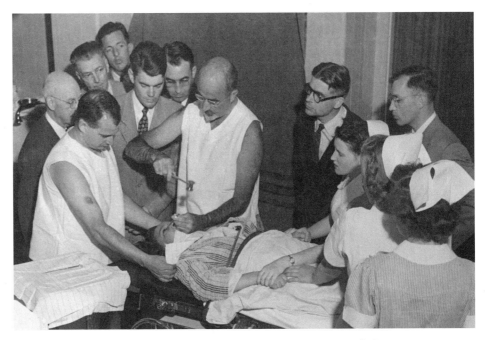

*Dr. Freeman performs a lobotomy surrounded
by colleagues interested in learning the procedure.*

prefrontal lobotomy, severed a series of nerves in the forward portion of the brain. Some surgeons reached the brain by drilling holes in the skull. Others entered through the eye sockets, using a sharp, slender instrument resembling an ice pick.

Though lobotomy reduced anxiety, it did so by damaging or destroying crucial areas of the brain. Some people became hostile and impulsive after the operation. Others lost their ability to speak or think clearly. Nevertheless, lobotomy was used until the mid-1950s. About 40,000 of these devastating surgeries were performed in the United States alone. Egas Moniz, who launched this era of "psychosurgery," was awarded the Nobel Prize for Medicine in 1949.

Most of the doctors who performed lobotomies were well-intentioned, though misguided. A far more sinister "treatment program" was conducted by psychiatrists in Nazi Germany.

During his rise to power in the 1930s Adolf Hitler gave impassioned speeches against "useless eaters," unproductive men and women who devoured the nation's limited resources. Hitler contended that mentally retarded persons and people with mental illnesses, confined to institutions, lived "lives unworthy of life." In 1940 Hitler authorized a program known as T-4, the "mercy killing" of chronic psychiatric patients. Groups of patients were transferred to designated hospitals for "evaluation." After a few weeks, they were ordered to take showers, where they were killed with poison gas. The T-4 program paved the way for the mass extermination of Jews, Gypsies, and other "undesirables" during the Nazi regime.

After World War II the American public began to awaken to the horrors of life in the nation's mental hospitals. Journalists such as Michael Gorman wrote shocking accounts of mistreatment and neglect. In 1946 a woman writing under the pen name Mary Jane Ward published an autobiographical novel based on her experiences as a patient in a New York state hos-

THE SNAKE PIT

Published in 1946, Mary Jane Ward's novel *The Snake Pit* became a motion picture in 1949. The book and the film raised public awareness about the horrors of American mental hospitals. In one scene the main character, dazed after a series of ECT treatments, ponders the attitudes of the staff: "It seemed to her that the hospital had no interest in teaching its patients to think. Juniper Hill's goal was to Keep Them Quiet. Perhaps a group of thinking patients would have disturbed the peace. Let people think and at once they are drawing up petitions and demanding Rights. There simply were not enough nurses to handle thinkers."[12]

pital. The hydrotherapy and shock treatments of the 1940s reminded Ward of the time-honored notion that a sudden jolt to the body or brain will jar the shattered mind back to reason. Reflecting upon rites at the ancient Greek temple at Delphi, she called her novel *The Snake Pit*.

BRAIN VS. MIND

Emil Kraepelin (1856–1926) took careful notes whenever he examined one of his psychiatric patients. Year by year he collected his notes on index cards that he stored in his office in Munich, Germany. Through his studies of patients, Kraepelin meticulously described two forms of severe mental disorder— manic-depressive illness and dementia praecox. Kraepelin found that patients with manic-depressive illness (known today as bipolar disorder) often improved and returned to productive, rewarding lives. He observed that patients with dementia praecox tended to deteriorate.

Kraepelin and Freud were born in the same year, and both became giants in the history of psychiatry. Yet their ideas and approaches were radically opposed to one another. Freud thought of symptoms as the expressions of unconscious wishes and repressed memories. Mental illness was the mind's response to a troubled past. To Kraepelin, on the other hand, psychiatric disorders were caused by abnormalities in the brain. Kraepelin lambasted Freud's "continual, relentless pushing for embarrassing sexual revelations,"[13] and Freud called Kraepelin a "coarse fellow."

There was no love lost between Freud and Kraepelin. Their differences were mirrored for decades in the work and writings of their followers. Until the 1960s most outpatient clinics were psychoanalytically oriented. Freud's principles were also invoked by many of the psychiatrists, psychologists, and social workers who staffed mental hospitals in the United States and Western Europe. At the same time, however, biologically

SPLIT PERSONALITIES

In 1911 a Swiss psychiatrist, Eugen Bleuler (1857–1939), advanced the term "schizophrenia," which replaced "dementia praecox." Schizophrenia comes from Greek words meaning "split" and "mind." The term refers to the person's inability to distinguish fantasy from reality. Bleuler also noted that schizophrenics often have inappropriate emotional reactions—they may laugh at a tragic accident or cry at a humorous movie.

People unfamiliar with the mental-health field sometimes believe that schizophrenia means "split personality," and confuse it with a very different psychiatric condition called multiple personality disorder (MPD). A person with MPD appears to have two or more completely separate personalities, each with his or her own name, talents, fears, motivations, and even handwriting. Often one personality does not know that the others exist. MPD was first described by physicians in the eighteenth century, but to this day it remains a mystery. Cases of MPD are portrayed in the movies *Sybil* (based on a book of the same name) and *The Three Faces of Eve*.

oriented doctors—those who regarded mental illnesses as brain diseases—treated their patients with insulin shock, ECT, and other physical methods.

Biological psychiatry argued that Freud's theories had no scientific basis. There were no statistics to prove that talking cures had any beneficial effects. The "talk therapists" claimed that biological psychiatry was cold and dehumanizing, that it reduced the complexities of the mind to mere chemical reactions.

The success of electroconvulsive therapy in the 1940s presented talk therapy with a major challenge. An electrical current through the brain could erase some of the most dramatic signs of mental illness. Surely this proved that mental illness resulted from the brain's malfunction. The Freudians countered that the convulsions of ECT symbolized the patient's inner struggles, and helped to liberate him from his unconscious conflicts. Talk treatments and ECT went on, sometimes almost side by side within the same hospital.

Then, in the early 1950s, a new medication was approved for use in the United States. The manufacturers claimed that it had marvelous calming effects on the most agitated patients. The new medication, chlorpromazine, was sold under the trade name Thorazine.

ACCENTUATE THE POSITIVE

A very different perspective on mental illnesses came from B. F. Skinner (1904–1990) and his followers, who called themselves "behaviorists." Skinner believed that all human behavior, even our thoughts and feelings, is caused by our reactions to reward and punishment. If our actions are rewarded with food, money, praise, or affection, we will continue or increase that particular behavior. If our actions are punished with pain, threats, or ostracism, we will change our behavior to avoid such consequences. Skinnerians refer to reward as "positive reinforcement," a pleasant result that encourages a particular behavior. Punishment, or "negative reinforcement," helps to extinguish a behavior.

According to Skinner, the bizarre or destructive behavior of people we consider mentally ill brings them rewards such as attention, stimulation, or comfort. Behavioral therapy positively reinforces desired behavior and extinguishes behavior that is undesirable. Skinner's approach has been used to alter the behavior of people with severe mental illnesses, and of children and teens who have emotional problems.

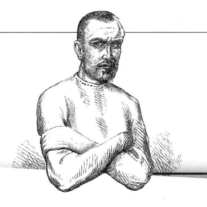

Chapter Eight

THE CHEMICAL REVOLUTION

I felt incapable of being angry about anything, irresistibly optimistic. . . . After about a week . . . my mood was of perfect euphoria, unaffected by the little traumas of daily life.

—Dr. Claudia Quarti,
who took Thorazine
as an experiment in 1952

THE FIRST BREAKTHROUGH

When a person is seriously injured, the body goes into a dangerous state known as shock. The blood pressure drops, the heart rate slows, and the person hovers on the brink of consciousness. When a patient is in deep shock, surgery is highly risky.

In the years after World War II a French naval surgeon named Henri Laborit began to search for a drug that would ease the effects of shock in surgical patients. At a naval hospital in Tunisia, Laborit developed a medication which he called 4560 R.P. The name was later changed to chlorpromazine.

Chlorpromazine had a remarkable calming effect on Laborit's patients. In 1952 Laborit wrote an article about his work and added, "These facts let us see certain indications for this drug in psychiatry."[1]

In the spring of 1952 two Paris psychiatrists tested chlorpromazine on a group of eight disturbed patients. One, whom they called Giovanni A., had been found roaming the streets with a pot of flowers on his head, giving speeches about the joys of liberty. After three weeks on chlorpromazine, Giovanni was calm, rational, and ready to leave the hospital. The other seven patients responded just as well.

Chlorpromazine reached the United States in 1952 under the auspices of the pharmaceutical firm Smith Klein & French. Dr. William Long, the firm's medical director, tried the new drug on five schizophrenic patients at a private hospital in Massachusetts. One of these patients was a nun who had come to the hospital shrieking and kicking in her distress. A colleague of Long's recalled: "[Long] was very concerned about the patient. He gave her some of this stuff. The results? He couldn't believe it! She had been extraordinarily abusive, with most unnunlike behavior. In the afternoon she was calm. He described it at the table in the lunchroom. What he described was a typical chlorpromazine result."[2]

SCHIZOPHRENIA ON DEMAND

Accounts from the seventeenth century describe epidemics of temporary madness that struck several villages in southern France. Today many scientists believe that these French peasants had eaten wheat tainted with ergot, a fungus that produces a toxic chemical called lysergic acid diethylamide. This compound, known today as LSD, heightens the senses, distorts thought processes, and triggers visual and auditory hallucinations. In the 1940s researchers synthesized LSD in the laboratory in order to study psychotic symptoms under experimental conditions. In the 1960s the Harvard-based psychologist Timothy Leary advocated the use of LSD by the general public, urging young people to "turn on and drop out." LSD and other hallucinogens became widely used "recreational drugs." If an LSD user was brought to the emergency room, terrified by the drug's effects, doctors gave him an injection of chlorpromazine to "bring him down."

Dr. Tim Leary, psychologist and social activist, used LSD in the belief that "To learn how to use your head, you have to go out of your mind."

Christening the new drug with the brand name Thorazine, Smith Klein & French launched a nationwide sales campaign in 1954. The marketing force targeted psychiatrists who worked in state and private hospitals. For the first time these doctors had a medication that brought peace to some of the most disturbed men and women in their care. Thorazine did not cure schizophrenia; if the patient stopped taking the drug her delusions and hallucinations were likely to return. Yet Thorazine brought patients into contact with the world again, and made life manageable in ways they had nearly forgotten. As one former patient explained, "It was like a chairman taking control of a meeting where everybody had been shouting at once."[3]

With the advent of Thorazine, hospital wards were transformed almost overnight. A staff member at a private hospital in Maryland described the change:

> The wild, screaming, unapproachable patient became a thing of the past. Many more patients could go for drives in the country, visit Towson or Baltimore for shopping excursions with or without attendants, go to the theater,

THE OTHER SIDE OF THE MIRACLE

At first Thorazine seemed to be a miracle treatment—effective, inexpensive, and harmless. Unlike ECT, it did not tear holes in a patient's memory. It did not leave her helpless and shattered, as did prefrontal lobotomy. But soon patients began to complain of a daunting array of side effects. Prolonged use of Thorazine causes dry mouth, drowsiness, and sensitivity to sunlight. Worse still, people who take the drug over several months or years often develop hand tremors and uncontrollable facial twitches. Some involuntarily thrust their tongues in and out of their mouths, licking their lips raw. Many walk with an awkward, dragging gait nicknamed "the Thorazine shuffle." These visible side effects may tag former patients with the stigma of mental illness when they try to return to society. Because of the social and physical discomfort of side effects, many patients take their medication irregularly or give it up altogether.

visit art museums, take in athletic contests, or go out with relatives for dinner. Life became more varied and interesting, and improvement was advanced.[4]

Thorazine did not work for all schizophrenic patients, but its success spurred drug companies to develop other psychiatric medications. By the late 1950s doctors could choose from a long list of antipsychotic drugs, experimenting with dosages and combinations for each individual patient. Yet schizophrenia was only one of the major mental illnesses that filled hospital beds. Researchers set to work to find chemical treatments for the other serious mental disorders as well.

TREATING THE UPS AND DOWNS

In March 1948, an Australian psychiatrist named John F. J. Cade injected lithium carbonate into one of his chronically ill patients. The patient was a fifty-year-old man who had been hospitalized for five years with manic-depressive illness, or bipolar disorder. His moods wavered up and down, from energetic "highs" to "lows" of withdrawal and misery. As Cade described him later: "He was amiably restless, dirty, destructive, mischievous and interfering. He had enjoyed preeminent nuisance value in a back ward for all those years and bid fair to remain there for the rest of his life."[5] Weeks after his first lithium injection, however, the man's moods had stabilized. He left the hospital and returned to his job.

Cade published his findings about lithium in an obscure Australian medical journal, where they went unnoticed for the next four years. Then, in 1952, a Danish researcher named Mogens Schou discovered Cade's work. Schou had a special interest in Cade's article. Several members of his family had bipolar disorder, and he had been hospitalized for the condi-

HITTING THE HEIGHTS

Kay Redfield Jamison is an internationally respected expert on bipolar disorder. She understands the condition from the inside, as she lives with it herself. In her autobiography she describes her dizzying peaks:

"With antennae perked, eyes fast-forwarding and fly-faceted, I took in everything around me. I was on the run. Not just on the run but first and foremost on the run, darting back and forth across the hospital parking lot trying to use up a boundless, relentless manic energy. I was running fast, but slowly going mad."[6]

tion himself. Eagerly Schou carried out a series of controlled experiments, some of the first to be conducted in the field of psychiatry. He gave lithium to one group of bipolar patients. To a comparable group he gave a placebo—a sugar pill with no medicinal value. None of the patients knew who was receiving which kind of pill. Schou's experiments showed that lithium had a dramatic impact on people with bipolar disorder. In the years that followed, lithium helped thousands of people in Europe, including Schou and his relatives, to remain healthy and productive. As Schou wrote, "Perhaps more than most scientists I have been granted the privilege of reaping the fruits of my labor."[7]

Despite glowing reports from across the Atlantic, the Food and Drug Administration (FDA) was reluctant to authorize the use of lithium in the United States. Many American doctors believed that lithium was dangerous. High doses caused kidney damage and heart problems, and some European patients had even died. Eventually, after lengthy deliberation, the FDA approved the use of lithium for people with bipolar disorder in 1970.

Far more widespread than manic-depressive illness is "unipolar" depression. People with this condition experience bouts of depression without manic highs at the other end of the scale. In 1955 a Swiss researcher named Roland Kuhn tested a new drug, imipramine, on forty severely depressed patients. "The patients became generally more lively," he wrote during the first weeks. "Their low depressive voices sound stronger. The patients appear more communicative. The yammering and crying came to an end. If the depression had manifested itself in a dissatisfied, plaintive, or irritable mood, a friendly, contented, and accessible spirit came to the fore."[8]

Imipramine was the first of the *tricyclic* antidepressant medications to come on the market. The tricyclics are so named

BRAIN MATTERS

Psychiatric medications affect mood swings, hallucinations, and anxiety levels by changing the chemical composition of the brain. Most "psychoactive drugs" raise or decrease the levels of chemicals called neurotransmitters. Neurotransmitters act as "chemical messengers," carrying impulses from one nerve cell to another. The three most important neurotransmitter systems that play a role in mental illnesses are norepinephrine, dopamine, and serotonin. At one time researchers believed that schizophrenia resulted from abnormal levels of dopamine in the brain, and that abnormal serotonin levels were responsible for mood disorders. More recent evidence suggests that the relationship between brain chemistry and mental illness is far more complex. Several neurotransmitters seem to work together in ways that are still only partially understood.

because the chemical structure of their molecules forms three circles. Pharmaceutical companies developed dozens of new tricyclic medications in the 1960s and 1970s. By the early 1980s psychiatrists in the United States wrote some ten million prescriptions for antidepressants per year.

Still another breakthrough came in the form of drugs to control anxiety. In the 1950s doctors began prescribing Librium, Valium, Miltown, and other antianxiety drugs to women and men who complained of excessive nervousness, fearfulness, and panic attacks. Often suggested for homemakers who were overwhelmed by the stresses of caring for small children and catering to demanding husbands, these "tranquilizers" were nicknamed "mother's little helpers." Tranquilizers became immensely popular in the 1950s and 1960s. By 1970, one out of five women and one of every thirteen men were using them at least occasionally. Many antianxiety drugs are habit-forming, and their overuse can lead to a whole new set of problems. In 1975 the FDA placed strict controls on prescriptions of Valium and similar drugs. Their use dropped off rapidly.

Another method of treating anxiety, developed in the 1950s, is known as "deconditioning," or "relaxation therapy." The person identifies a situation that triggers his anxiety, such as riding in an elevator. First the therapist teaches him a set of relaxation techniques, such as deep breathing. Then the therapist gives him a series of exercises involving elevators, and asks him to use the relaxation techniques during each one. The patient may be told to look at pictures of an elevator, then to watch people entering a real elevator. Next he might step into a stationary elevator with the door standing open. Finally he is ready to take an actual elevator ride. Deconditioning is very effective for people with phobias or intense fears of specific objects or situations.

RETHINKING MENTAL ILLNESSES

Thorazine, lithium, imipramine, and other psychoactive drugs transformed the lives of people with mental illness. At the same time, they radically changed the field of psychiatry. Treatments such as lobotomy and insulin therapy dropped out of favor. Straitjackets, cold packs, and other physical restraints fell into disuse. With the proper medication most patients quickly became quiet and manageable.

But to some dedicated psychoanalysts, drug therapies were anathema. The Freudians argued that medications merely masked the patient's symptoms and made it more difficult to uncover the roots of his problem. Drugs did not cure mental illness; the symptoms usually flooded back as soon as the patient stopped taking the pills. "If they have to get addicted, I would rather see them addicted to psychotherapy than to drugs," declared Dr. Elvin Semrad of the Massachusetts Mental Health Center. "When you take poison, sooner or later you get poisoned. And all drugs are poison."[9]

The doctors who worked in mental hospitals treating schizophrenics and other severely ill patients shrugged this argument aside. Psychoanalysis was a painfully slow process, they pointed out, and its benefits had never been scientifically proven. Hospital patients needed help here and now. Medication relieved their suffering and enabled them to live fuller lives. The analysts lived in an "ivory tower," treating mildly troubled people who hardly needed help in the first place. Responding to this debate, an article in *Time* magazine concluded,

> The ivory-tower critics argue that the red-brick [mental hospital] pragmatists are not getting to the patient's underlying psychopathology, and so there can be no cure. These

doctors want to know whether he withdrew from the world because of unconscious conflicts or incestuous urges or stealing from his brother's piggybank at the age of five. In the world of red-bricks, this is like arguing about the number of angels on the head of a pin.[10]

From the outset of the chemical revolution, however, many analysts saw the benefits of medication for their patients. Over time, talk therapy and psychopharmacology (drug-based therapy) drifted toward a truce. Most psychiatrists and other mental-health professionals came to believe that medication was an invaluable treatment tool. It was nearly impossible to do talk therapy with a patient who was distracted by threatening voices or soaring on the delusion that he was about to take charge of the United Nations. With medication, however, the voices faded, the delusions disappeared, and the patient was better able to talk about his life—past, present, and future.

In a sense, the development of drug treatments revived a view of madness that prevailed in the eighteenth century. In the days before moral treatment, alienists believed that mental illnesses were diseases of the brain, to be treated by bringing the humors into balance. In the 1950s doctors again found biological underpinnings in major mental illnesses. This time they used drugs that had been tested in scientific laboratories and approved by the federal government. Instead of balancing the humors, the new medications sought to balance neurotransmitters within the brain. In the 1760s and the 1960s the goal was the same—to restore the patient's equilibrium and to make him fit for life in society.

As more and more medications came onto the market, psychiatrists faced a fresh set of problems. How could they decide which patient should receive which drug or combination of drugs? In the case of physical disease, such decisions were fairly

THE PSYCHIATRIC BIBLE

In 1952 a group of psychiatrists compiled a slender volume that they called the *Diagnostic and Statistical Manual of Mental Disorders* (DSM.) The DSM contained short descriptions of a variety of mental illnesses, and was designed to help doctors and other professionals diagnose their child and adult patients. A greatly enlarged version of the book, DSM II, appeared in 1968. DSM IV, published in 1994, is a massive 942-page tome, bulging with descriptions of more than 300 conditions.

Over the years the DSM has been a source of intense controversy. Its creators have been accused of pathologizing everyday life—that is, putting diagnostic labels on emotional reactions that seem to fall well within the normal range. A person who struggles to quit smoking may be diagnosed with "nicotine dependence." A boy who disturbs his fifth-grade class may be said to have an "oppositional defiant personality disorder." Furthermore, diagnoses in the DSM sometimes have serious political implications. In 1974 gay and lesbian groups successfully lobbied to have homosexuality removed from the DSM's list of mental illnesses. Vietnam veterans fought to have the condition known as post-traumatic stress disorder (PTSD) included, so that people with this condition could be reimbursed by insurance companies for treatment.

straightforward. Doctors made a careful diagnosis and pre-scribed drugs known to combat the illness in question. But the diagnosis of mental illnesses had always been an inexact science, its rules ever shifting and blurring. This fuzziness was no longer acceptable. Now, as they edged closer to "hard science," mental-health professionals became increasingly concerned with labels and classifications. What was the real difference between schizophrenia and mania? When was a person clinically depressed, as opposed to merely sad or discouraged? What was the dividing line between anxiety disorder and the ordinary emotional stress of daily life? What, in fact, constituted mental illness, and what was mental health?

Chapter Nine

UNBOLTING
THE
GATES

If you really want to know about discharge planning, go to the Round Table Pizza around the corner. There's a table in the back that has a lot of the patients who've been here already and a lot of the others who haven't been here yet.

— A mental-health worker
at a county hospital
in Berkeley, California, 1995

MADNESS AND MYTH

The 1960s were a decade of questions and challenges. Americans took to the streets to protest their government's involvement in a war in Southeast Asia. African Americans, women, and gays fought for equal rights. Old rules crumbled, and new voices clamored to be heard.

In 1961 a sociologist named Erving Goffman published a study comparing prison inmates with patients in mental hospitals. Both were held against their will, deprived of their civil rights, and forced to follow an institution's grinding routine. Goffman wrote that on admission, "the recruit begins a series of abasements, degradations, humiliations, and profanations of self. His self is systematically, if often unintentionally, mortified."[1]

The following year Ken Kesey's best-selling novel, *One Flew over the Cuckoo's Nest* drew a scathing portrait of abusive authorities in a psychiatric hospital. In the book Randall McMurphy, a lifelong rebel, feigns madness to avoid a prison sentence. McMurphy asks only to "just play poker and stay single and live where and how he wants to, if people would let him," he says. "But you know how society persecutes a dedicated man."[2] After a series of confrontations with the sinister ward nurse, McMurphy is forced into submission with a prefrontal lobotomy.

Goffman and Kesey spoke from the outskirts of the "antipsychiatry movement," which gathered momentum during the 1960s. Challenging the very premises of mental-health treatment, the movement sprang up within the profession of psychiatry itself. In 1960 Thomas Szasz, a Hungarian-born psychoanalyst, published a highly controversial book called *The Myth of Mental Illness*. Szasz contended that psychiatric illnesses do not really exist. He argued that society has constructed the notion of mental illness in order to label and segregate trouble-

Film still of Jack Nicholson (second from right) and supporting actor Danny Devito (left) in One Flew Over the Cuckoo's Nest

some individuals who refuse to conform. Psychiatric treatment, Szasz explained, is society's way of forcing rebels into the mold.

In another book, *The Manufacture of Madness* (1970), Szasz finds parallels between the Inquisition of medieval Europe and modern psychiatric practices. The psychiatrist tries to unveil the secret thoughts of the patient, and the inquisitor sought to reveal the hidden thoughts of the accused. The psychiatrist looks for symptoms, and the inquisitor searched for witch's marks. The persecution of witches was profitable for church authorities, and the treatment of mental patients is profitable for psychiatrists. Once a person was accused of witchcraft, the inquisitor would work relentlessly to prove his guilt. Once a per-

THE HELPING PROFESSIONS

Psychiatrists, psychologists, psychoanalysts, clinical social workers—what are the differences among the many professions that treat people who have mental illnesses? A psychiatrist is a medical doctor (M.D.) who specializes in mental disorders. Psychiatrists can do "talk therapy," and can also prescribe medications. A psychoanalyst is a psychiatrist who has additional training in psychoanalytically oriented therapy. A psychologist may have a master's (M.A.) or doctorate (Ph.D.), but does not undergo medical training. Psychologists can provide various kinds of psychotherapy and are trained to administer personality and intelligence tests. A clinical social worker has a master's or doctorate in social work (M.S.W. or D.S.W.), and can also do psychotherapy. Other helping professionals, most of whom work in hospitals or clinics, include psychiatric nurses, art therapists, and music therapists.

son enters psychiatric treatment, he is almost automatically branded "mentally ill." "In more than twenty years of psychiatric work," Szasz wrote, "I have never known a clinical psychologist to report, on the basis of a projective test, that the subject is a normal, mentally healthy person. . . . There is no behavior or person that a modern psychiatrist cannot plausibly diagnose as abnormal or ill."[3]

Another renegade voice came from the British psychiatrist Ronald David (R.D.) Laing (1927–1989). Laing's 1960 work, *The Divided Self*, set forth a new theory of schizophrenia. According to Laing, schizophrenia is a sane response to a mad world. The schizophrenic may be the most sensitive member of a disturbed family, the one who is forced into retreat by the destructive behavior that surrounds him. At times Laing's writings seem to glorify schizophrenia, claiming that the mad have special courage and insights.

"Perhaps we will learn to accord to so-called schizophrenics who have come back to us, perhaps after years, no less respect than [we give] the often no less lost explorers of the Renaissance. Future generations will see that what we call schizophrenia was one of the forms which, through often quite ordinary people, the light begins to break through the cracks in our all too closed minds."[4]

Traditional psychiatrists were outraged by Szasz, Laing, and others in the antipsychiatry camp. They argued that mental illnesses are real illnesses that cause untold suffering, and can be treated effectively with medication and talk therapy. Joanne

KINGSLEY HALL

During the 1960s R.D. Laing and his colleagues treated several persons, all with the "schizophrenia label," at a London mansion called Kingsley Hall. In the past Kingsley Hall had been a residence for political radicals, including the revolutionary Indian leader Mohandas Gandhi. Now it served as the testing ground for a revolutionary approach to mental illness. Residents of Kingsley Hall were allowed to regress to an infantile state in which all their needs were met by the staff. Laing believed this regression would permit the person with schizophrenia to begin again, to "grow up" healthy and whole.

During her sojourn at Kingsley Hall, forty-two-year-old Mary Barnes spent months lying in bed, soiling herself and sucking from baby bottles. "Much of me was twisted and buried and turned in upon itself as a tangled skein of wool to which the end had been lost," she wrote later. "The big muddle started before I was born. It went on getting worse. . . . What I was trying to do was to get back inside my mother, to be reborn, to come up again straight and clear of all the mess."[5] Mary Barnes recovered, left Kingsley Hall, and became an acclaimed painter.

Greenberg, a novelist and the survivor of a severe mental illness, was appalled by Laing's idealization of schizophrenia. "Creativity and mental illness are opposites, and not complements," she protested in an interview. "I want to choose my perceptions. I don't want them to come out of some kind of unconscious soup. I want it to be something I choose to say, not something that says me."[6]

The antipsychiatry movement heightened public concern about the conditions in mental hospitals and the coercive treatment of patients with drugs, lobotomy, and ECT. At the same time, a number of popular books and films depicted the healing of troubled minds by skilled and caring psychiatrists and other professionals. The 1962 movie *David and Lisa* is the moving story of two emotionally disturbed teens who meet in a psychiatric hospital. Joanne Greenberg's autobiographical novel *I Never Promised You a Rose Garden* (published under the pseudonym Hannah Greene) recounts the successful treatment of a schizophrenic girl by a gifted therapist, Dr. Fried. Works such as these helped sustain the public's faith in mental-health care and fostered a sense of hope for people with mental illnesses.

DREAMS AND DISILLUSION

"I propose a national mental-health program to assist in the inauguration of a wholly new emphasis and approach to care for the mentally ill," proclaimed President John F. Kennedy in February 1963. "Government at every level, . . . private foundations and individual citizens must all face up to their responsibilities in this area. We need to return mental-health care to the mainstream of American medicine."[7] In the second half of the 1960s Kennedy's nationwide mental-health policy sprang into life. Hundreds of millions of federal, state, and municipal dollars

I NEVER PROMISED YOU A ROSE GARDEN

In her 1964 novel, Joanne Greenberg drew upon her experiences as a patient at Chestnut Lodge, a private hospital in Maryland. Deborah Blau, the novel's protagonist, has created an inner world called Yr, a world with its own laws, gods, and language.

> Sometimes she was able to see "reality" from Yr as if the partition between the two were only gauze. On such occasions her name became Januce, because she felt like two-faced Janus—with a face on either world. It had been her letting slip this name which had caused the first trouble in school. . . . The teacher had said, "Deborah, what is this mark on your paper? What is this word, Januce?" And, as the teacher stood by her desk, some nightmare terror coming to life had risen in the day-sane schoolroom. Deborah had looked about and found that she could not see except in outlines, gray against gray, and with no depth, but flatly, like a picture. The mark on the paper was the emblem of coming from Yr's time to Earth's, but, being caught while still in transition, she had to answer for both of them.[8]

poured into a set of programs under the umbrella of "community mental health."

The community mental-health movement has its roots in nineteenth-century Germany. During the 1860s a few German asylums created "open wards," where patients came and went of their own free will. Upon discharge, many boarded with families in the community. In 1930 the Mental Health Act established similar hospitals in Great Britain. In 1939 Britain's Runwell Hospital pioneered a social club for former patients. Run almost entirely by patients themselves, the club sponsored discussions, outings, and a magazine.

GHEEL REVISITED

At the dawn of the twenty-first century, the Belgian town of Gheel was still a haven for people with chronic mental illness. By then the government paid stipends to families that took patients into their homes, and professionals screened patients for this special foster-care program. Nevertheless, the spirit of Gheel remained as welcoming as it had been for the past six hundred years. No matter how odd their appearance or behavior, people with mental illnesses were fully accepted as members of the community.

Matthew Dumont, a Boston psychiatrist, studied Gheel for several years, and noted the positive impact of mentally ill persons on the whole town. "You would not see a person lying in the street, homeless, in Gheel," he states. "There would be a sense of responsibility for that person. . . . A population that treats the mentally ill with such acceptance, with such tolerance, is a tolerant community. It's a community defined by its inclusiveness rather than its exclusiveness, and I think that's beautiful."[9]

In the United States, several factors combined to launch the community mental-health movement. The antipsychiatry writings of Szasz and others led the public to question the wisdom of locking people away just because their behavior was odd or annoying. Furthermore, horrifying reports in the popular press exposed the atrocities of life on the wards of public and private institutions. "No matter how bad it is for those people on the streets," stated journalist Michael Gorman, "it's better than it was in the hospitals."[10] With medications to control their symptoms, patients could be discharged from hospitals more quickly than ever before. There seemed no need to keep them behind locked gates when they would be better off on the outside.

The basic premise of community mental health was to provide psychiatric services to people outside of the hospital setting. Psychiatrists would oversee medications on an outpatient basis. An assortment of professionals—psychiatrists, psychologists, and social workers—would provide group and individual psychotherapy. In addition there would be social activities, job-placement services, and counseling for patients' family members. By the late 1980s, 789 community mental-health centers were operating with federal funds. They offered help to people in nearly every U.S. county.

At the same time the centers were opening, state hospitals were closing their doors. State officials pressured hospitals to close their back wards by discharging chronic patients, some of whom had lived there for decades. Most such patients had completely lost touch with family and friends, and had forgotten how to function in the outside world. The process of releasing these long-term patients was known as "deinstitutionalization." Hospitals and legislators assumed that the community mental-health system could help these men and women adjust successfully to the confusing demands of life beyond the hospital walls. But within a few short years, journalists, hospital staff, and patients themselves gave deinstitutionalization a new name. They referred to it as "dumping."

Meanwhile, hospital stays for new admissions grew shorter and shorter. Hospitals focused on starting the patient on antipsychotic or antidepressant drugs, or changing the dosage of a previous medication. There was little time for psychotherapy. There was hardly time to talk to the patient about where he would go when he left the hospital again. Unless he was clearly "dangerous to himself or others," the goal was to stabilize the patient as quickly as possible and send him on his way. There wasn't enough staff to care for long-term patients. There weren't enough beds.

Tragically, the flow of government money for community mental-health programs soon dwindled to a trickle. Even well-funded centers had trouble recruiting qualified staff willing to work with people who were poor and severely ill. More and more outpatient clinics began to treat "the worried well," middle-class clients who could pay handsomely for the therapeutic hour. Those in the greatest need of help were left to fend for themselves.

Without the encouragement of family or professionals, many ex-patients stopped taking their medications. Swelling the ranks of the homeless, they slept in parks or under bridges, panhandled for change, and wandered the streets talking to invisible companions. The hospital was no longer a refuge. If a disturbed man was admitted, by choice or under police escort, he could not expect to stay for more than a week or two. E. Fuller Torrey, author of numerous books on mental-health issues, commented, "It was as if a policy of resettlement had been agreed upon, but only eviction took place."[11]

In May 1981, *Life* magazine printed a gut-wrenching article, complete with photographs, on the plight of the homeless mentally ill. It described William Hopkins of Springfield, Massachusetts, "hallucinating between fleeting moments of clarity, butting his head against store windows, pounding his forehead until it bleeds."[12] Neil deLuck, who had been hospitalized twenty-nine times, lived in an unheated attic. He had not changed his clothes for two months, and was covered with body lice.

BACK TO THE SHIP OF FOOLS?

During the 1980s New York City considered a proposal to create "floating shelters" for the homeless mentally ill. The city would use "surplus troop ships, ocean liners, oil rigs, or barges . . . moored at waterfront piers" as makeshift housing. If citizens near one pier complained, the ship could sail off to another site."[13]

By the 1990s, it was estimated that one-third of the homeless people in the United States had severe mental illnesses.

For many discharged patients, however, the situation was far more hopeful. Some moved into "halfway houses" on the grounds of a hospital. In a halfway house, patients were free from most hospital restrictions. They could shop, socialize, and go out to work. Mental-health workers were on staff twenty-four hours a day. Some towns and cities opened group homes for former patients. As many as a dozen men and women shared a house, with mental-health workers living on the premises or stopping by each day to be sure everything ran smoothly. Such programs, far less costly than hospital care, offered people with mental illnesses a combination of self-direction and emotional support. A *New York Times* reporter described a group home in Glen Cove, Long Island: "No one wears a uniform or walks around with keys on his belt. Staff and residents dress informally, in street clothes. If a stranger were suddenly dropped in the middle of the house, it's unlikely he'd figure out where he was."[14]

WHICH SIDE ARE YOU ON?

On June 26, 1975, the United States Supreme Court ruled in a landmark case called *Donaldson* v. *Florida State Hospital*. Kenneth Donaldson, who had schizophrenia, was hospitalized against his will at Florida State for fifteen years. He wrote endless letters to relatives, reporters, lawyers, and legislators, until he rallied a group of staunch supporters who took his case to the highest court in the nation.

Ironically, Donaldson's bid for freedom was based on the argument that the hospital violated his right to treatment. Since the hospital failed to provide him with even minimal psychotherapy, it had no right to hold him as a patient. The Supreme Court ruled in Donaldson's favor. The final decision declares that "a state cannot constitutionally confine without treatment a nondangerous individual who is capable of surviving safely in freedom by himself or with the help of willing and responsible family members or friends."[15] The Court explained: "The mere presence of mental illness does not disqualify a person from preferring his home to the comforts of an institution."[16]

After Donaldson won his release, he joined a growing band of lawyers and ex-patients who campaigned for reform in the laws governing psychiatric hospitalization. The American Civil Liberties Union (ACLU), the Mental Health Law Project, and other organizations worked to change the laws regarding commitment and the involuntary use of medications and ECT. By the mid 1980s, several states forbade hospitals to require patients to take medication. New commitment laws made it illegal to hold any patient against her will for more than seventy-two hours unless she was dangerous to herself or others. Patients were to be treated in "the least restrictive setting possible."

Mental-health activists celebrated the new regulations, which they believed would cut down on the abuses suffered by Kenneth Donaldson and thousands of others. But most professionals in the mental-health field were appalled. Mental illness interfered with a person's ability to make rational choices, they argued. How could a severely paranoid man, convinced that CIA agents were trying to poison him, make a reasonable decision about taking Thorazine? How could a woman in the grip of mania, sure that she was about to win the Nobel Prize, be persuaded to take lithium for her own good? When patients refused treatment and left the hospital, all too often they ended up sleeping in doorways or curled up on heating grates in the sidewalk. As one doctor put it, "A large number of patients have been kidnapped by a small number of lawyers in order to make a philosophical point on their own behalf."[17]

A number of politicians and mental-health professionals, E. Fuller Torrey among them, argue in favor of involuntary medication. If this policy were enacted, persons with severe mental illness could be medicated against their will, for their own good and for the good of society. The debate gains media attention whenever a former mental patient is involved in a violent crime. Only a small fraction of the mentally ill population has violent tendencies, but highly publicized cases fan deep-seated fears.

Ironically, many of the patients liberated from institutions quickly fell prey to the judicial system. A 1993 survey found that about 200,000 persons with mental illness were being held in jails and prisons nationwide. Most had committed misdemeanors—loitering, panhandling, or disturbing the peace. They needed psychiatric treatment, not sentencing. But no treatment was available. They were locked into cells like criminals to get them off the streets. Homeless shelters in U.S. cities became refuges for thousands of former psychiatric patients in the 1970s. Like the almshouses of the nineteenth century, these shelters became catchall institutions for alcoholics, petty criminals, abuse victims, and people with severe mental illnesses.

In the 1980s and 1990s mental-health workers noted that more and more patients had "dual diagnoses"—that is, their schizophrenia or bipolar disorder was compounded by substance abuse. Psychiatric hospitals were not equipped to deal with people with alcoholism or heroin addiction. Drug-treatment centers could not cope with the delusions and disordered thinking of schizophrenia. Many people with the combination of mental illness and substance abuse wound up in prison cells.

By the turn of the millennium, many mental-health professionals and patients were deeply pessimistic about mental-health care in the United States. Yet the millennium witnessed some hopeful trends. New drugs and new ideas opened a brighter future for people with mental illnesses.

Chapter Ten

WHERE DO WE GO FROM HERE?

What is mentalism? It's the weeding away of ourselves from ourselves, the enforcement of who we are supposed to be instead of who we are, the glorification of pretense and the denial of our humanity. It is the denial of our abilities to perceive, think, decide, act, feel, and release emotions. It is the denial of our ability to understand ourselves in new ways and to change our lives and our world.

—Janet Foner,
a mental patient/activist

THE GEOGRAPHY OF THE PSYCHE

During the 1990s the National Institute of Mental Health (NIMH) conducted a series of studies on teenagers who had recently been diagnosed with schizophrenia. The researchers used a new technique called magnetic resonance imaging (MRI) to create detailed pictures of the young people's brains. They compared these brain images with those of healthy teens of the same ages. The MRI results showed that the brains of the teens with schizophrenia were smaller than those of the healthy control subjects. The ventricles (open spaces within the brain) of the schizophrenics were larger, as were the sulci, or wrinkles on the brain's outer layer. This outer layer, called the cortex, was thinner in the teens with schizophrenia than it was in the teens who did not have the disorder.

Other researchers compared the brain activity of schizo-phrenics and nonschizophrenics as they carried out a variety of simple tasks: recalling lists of words, looking at pictures, sniffing pleasant and unpleasant odors, identifying the direction of a sound, tapping out a rhythm with their fingers. The schizo-phrenics showed unusual neurological activity in several areas of their brains, especially the thalamus. In the normal brain the thalamus serves as a kind of filter, screening out unwanted information such as background noise. Scientists suspect that in schizophrenics the thalamus fails to regulate input such as sounds and sights, causing the mind to go into "overload."

A number of studies suggest that schizophrenia has a genetic component. If one parent has schizophrenia, each child in the family has a 10 percent chance of developing the condition. The risk factor rises to 40 percent if both parents are schizophrenic. The records of identical twins yielded interesting findings. If one twin develops schizophrenia, the other twin has a 40 percent chance of having the disease as well. Since identical twins have

GAZING WITHIN

Until late in the twentieth century, scientists collected much of their information about the brain by observing people who had survived strokes or head injuries. By studying the resulting changes in a person's abilities and temperament they learned the role of various areas of the brain. Today researchers have far more precise methods for studying the brain, using highly sophisticated "brain imaging" techniques. Brain imaging technologies include magnetic resonance imaging (MRI), the computer axial tomography (CAT scan), and positron emission tomography (PET scan). Through the use of these techniques researchers can view the brain in action. They can chart which areas are active or dormant during particular tasks, and which are awakened by specific emotions.

With these astounding new developments, human beings are making extraordinary gains in understanding the workings of the brain. Yet we are only at the beginning. We are not even close to unlocking the physiology of consciousness, the chemistry of thought, and the mysteries of that vast, unfathomable region of the mind we call the unconscious. In a sense, our passion to unmask the workings of the brain is a quest to know ourselves, but every answer only brings us a new set of questions.

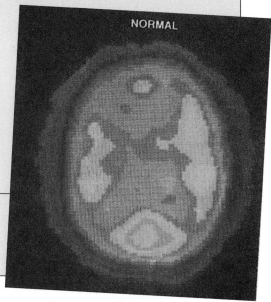

One of the first PET scans, introduced to the public in a Newsweek *article in 1980.*

exactly the same genes, these data imply that genes alone do not produce schizophrenia. Birth injuries to the brain, viruses, and stress may also contribute to the onset of the condition.

The ancient Greeks and the physicians of the eighteenth century thought madness was due to disease in the brain. The

HELLO, MY WORDS!

Joseph D'Agostino, a schizophrenic patient in a Boston hospital, spent his days filling page after page with frenzied writing. To most people his tangled strings of words were meaningless nonsense. But psychologist Lauren Slater suspected that D'Agostino was trying desperately to convey real thoughts and stories, which became lost beneath the heaps of irrelevant words he could not filter out. When Slater studied and edited D'Agostino's work, she uncovered clear, straightforward communication. Where he wrote, "Going back to school is a keyboard to the excellence exciting and I want to walk down the paths to the black flag beating blackboard," Slater revealed, "Going back to school is exciting. I want to walk to the blackboard." Slater gathered several of D'Agostino's jumbled stories and pruned them carefully. He gazed in wonder at the typewritten pages and murmured, "Hello, my words!"[1]

most recent research on schizophrenia bears out this belief. It banishes the notion that bad parenting causes schizophrenia, or that the illness is a sane person's response to a crazy world. Schizophrenia has profound effects upon the mind—upon thought, perception, and emotion. But it is a disease with its physical origin in the chemistry and tissues of the brain.

Research on mood disorders—major depression and bipolar, or manic-depressive, illness—has also had promising results. Like schizophrenia, mood disorders seem to run in families. If a parent has bipolar disorder, there is a 30 percent chance that the disease will appear in each child. Interestingly, researchers have found that both types of mood disorder often appear in the same family. This suggests that bipolar and unipolar disorders

GENIUS AND MADNESS

In 1994 a brilliant mathematician named John Forbes Nash Jr. received the Nobel Prize in Economic Sciences. His pioneering work in an area called "game theory" was a major contribution to the fields of economics and international policy. Game theory is a mathematically based explanation of competition. Nash was the first Nobel laureate with a diagnosis of schizophrenia. His story, captured in the award-winning 2002 feature film *A Beautiful Mind*, shows that people with severe mental illnesses can recover and live rewarding, productive lives. It also highlights the little-understood link that sometimes exists between mental illness and creativity.

An unusual number of highly creative people—including the physicist Albert Einstein and writers James Joyce and Bertrand Russell—had children with schizophrenia. In addition, the children of schizophrenic parents have a higher-than-average tendency to become writers or artists. The link between creativity and mood disorders is even stronger. One study of thirty writers found that 80 percent of them had a history of depression or bipolar disorder. Many of the writers' relatives also had mood disorder, high creativity, or both at once.

John Forbes Nash Jr.

are genetically related. Furthermore, if one identical twin has a mood disorder, the likelihood that the other twin will also have a mood disorder is 65 percent.

Little by little, researchers are unraveling the complex relationship between mood disorders and brain chemistry. In 1970 Julius Axelrod, a scientist at NIMH, won the Nobel Prize in

Medicine for his work on the effects of imipramine. Axelrod discovered that imipramine and other tricyclic antidepressants increased the level of norepinephrine, one of the neurotransmitters active in the brain. Other antidepressant medications were found to increase the availability of another neurotransmitter, serotonin. The discovery of the role of serotonin in depression led to the development of a series of new drugs called "selective serotonin re-uptake inhibitors," or SSRIs. The best known of these is a medication called Prozac. The most recent findings suggest that all three neurotransmitter sys-

HAPPINESS PLUS

After thirteen years of testing, the FDA approved Prozac for use as an antidepressant in 1987. Prozac had fewer side effects than earlier antidepressant medications, and gave its users a glowing sense of well-being. In addition it led to weight loss without dieting. Extravagant claims about the drug's benefits swept the media. By 1990 millions of Americans were taking Prozac regularly, and thousands more were begging their doctors for prescriptions.

Prozac appealed not only to people with debilitating major depression. It found a voracious market also within the general population. Nearly everyone feels sad from time to time—over an academic failure, a disastrous business deal, or a lost love. Prozac promised to relieve the sadness that is part of human life, and to lift its users to a state a few notches better than normal. Editorials heralded Prozac as the first "cosmetic drug," a drug to help healthy people feel even more well. By the late 1990s, however, the public realized that Prozac did not work miracles after all, and the fad subsided. Used responsibly, Prozac and similar drugs can be very helpful in combating depression.

THE FOOTPRINTS OF MENTAL TRAUMA

In support of the theory of neural plasticity, imaging techniques are beginning to show structural changes in the brains of people with post-traumatic stress disorder (PTSD). People with PTSD, such as the survivors of war or physical and sexual abuse, appear to have alterations in the cerebral cortex, the part of the brain involved in reasoning and social awareness. They also have changes in the limbic system, which governs anger, fear, and other emotions. These structural changes may account for some of the symptoms of PTSD, such as aggressiveness, hostility, and poor impulse control.

tems—dopamine, serotonin, and norepinephrine—are involved in mood disorders and schizophrenia.

Yet by its very nature the brain is infinitely responsive to experience and perception. Freud and his followers recognized that frightening or painful childhood experiences had lasting effects on the mind. With little knowledge of brain physiology they based the practice of psychotherapy upon their observations of troubled men, women, and children. In the 1970s researchers found biological evidence to help explain the impact of trauma. They showed that the brain is constantly changing, and that its chemistry shifts in direct response to stressful events. These chemical variations lead to structural changes in the brain itself. Brain cells move, rearrange themselves, grow, and die in ways that are influenced by the experiences in each individual's life. This concept is called the "theory of neural plasticity."

The overwhelming weight of genetic and biochemical research proves that major mental illnesses are brain diseases. Based on this evidence many hospitals and managed-care companies argue that these conditions should simply be treated with drugs. The right dosage of the proper pill should eliminate the patient's symptoms and return her to a normal state of mind. With funding cutbacks and staff shortages at most hospitals and outpatient clinics, talk therapy is often viewed as a needless luxury, a futile experiment whose time has passed. The director of one Florida health maintenance organization (HMO) referred to psychotherapy jeeringly as "Rent-a-Friend."[2]

Balancing the brain's chemistry is crucial. But a growing number of studies demonstrate that the best outcomes for patients occur when they receive a combination of drugs and psychotherapy. Nothing can replace the warmth and wisdom of a caring human being. A good relationship with a therapist can offer the gift that is utterly critical in any healing process—the gift of hope. Dan Fisher, a research chemist who has been hospitalized due to schizophrenia, explains that having another person believe in him helped him believe in himself. Addressing a group of former patients, Fisher said: "Darkness comes to us again and again, as do fears, failures, and wipeouts. The obstacles to recovery are numerous, but the greatest obstacle of all is simply that most people think that one cannot recover."[3]

Genes and chemicals, complex as they are, cannot account for the enormous depth and variety of human emotions—the richness of friendship, the sustaining power of love, the anguish of grief, the agonizing torment of moral conflict. Psychotherapy explores the multiple layers of human experience, both outer and inner. It reveals the hidden corners of memory, discovers patterns and parallels, makes sense of contradictions, and affirms the uniqueness and value of each individual. Through psychotherapy a troubled individual can learn more effective ways to cope with anger, stress, worry, and fear.

Preliminary research suggests that talk treatments may actually change the chemistry of the brain. Just as mental trauma has a harmful biological impact, positive experiences seem to have beneficial effects. The positive experience of connecting with a therapist, of feeling free to share one's innermost feelings, to be heard without judgment or penalty, may bring about healthy alterations at the brain's chemical and structural level. Generations of therapists and patients have insisted that talking treatments make a real difference. At last we have some data that begin to explain how and why.

OLD PROBLEMS, NEW LIVES

In December 2001, mental-health professionals, psychiatric patients, and their families sent thousands of letters and e-mail messages to their representatives in the U.S. Congress. A congressional committee was debating about "parity," an issue crucial to people with mental illnesses. The term parity refers to the way insurance companies cover medical costs for mental and physical disorders. Most companies offer extensive lifetime coverage for physical diseases, but very limited reimbursement for the treatment of schizophrenia, mood disorders, and other forms of mental illness. A proposed law would have changed all that, guaranteeing parity, or equality, in coverage for all illnesses alike.

Despite the tireless efforts of the mental-health community, a joint congressional committee voted to drop the proposed parity amendment. The decision reflected the prejudice of insurance companies, who don't want to pay for the treatment of an illness that is "all in the patient's head." It was also a reflection of the social stigma that has been attached to mental illness since the days of exorcism for demonic possession.

Among the strongest advocates for parity legislation is the National Alliance for the Mentally Ill (NAMI), largely composed of the relatives of mentally ill persons. In a press release on December 18, 2001, NAMI's executive director, Richard C.

Birkel, wrote: "Mental illnesses are brain disorders. They are as much physical illnesses as heart disease, diabetes, or epilepsy. Congress should not be abandoning the millions of people who battle severe mental illnesses every year." Lamenting the defeat of the 2001 parity amendment, Birkel added: "Our consolation comes in this promise: parity will not go away. If our leaders fail, we will hold them accountable—every time a family faces a crisis or is plunged into grief. Every time insurance discrimination kills, we will ask them again: whom do they really represent? We will be back. And next time, the majority will win."[4]

In April 2002, President George W. Bush made a strong statement supporting parity legislation. Bush also appointed a fifteen-member New Freedom Commission on Mental Health to study the strengths and weaknesses of the mental-health system and to recommend ways of improving services to consumers.

The 2001 fight for parity united psychiatrists and family members with patients themselves in pursuit of a common cause. Patients and former patients wrote letters, marched on picket lines, and spoke eloquently to reporters. They told the public who they were, and recounted their personal histories.

Since the 1940s people with mental illnesses have gathered for social activities and discussions. Most of these "social clubs" or "aftercare groups" were run by social workers or other professionals. But in the early 1970s patients in cities across the United States began to meet on their own, without professional supervision. They shared their experiences at various hospitals and clinics. They spoke of their struggles to find housing and work. They talked openly about mental illness itself, with all its fear, uncertainty, and despair.

Here and there leaders began to emerge—women and men who had been through "the system" and wanted to see real changes. These new mental-patient activists believed that the people best equipped to help were those who had lived through

A NAME FOR PREJUDICE

The term "mentalism" arose in the mental-patients' movement to describe the attitude that people with mental illnesses are damaged, inferior beings who need to be fixed. Mentalism labels people, stuffs them into categories, and strips them of their basic humanity. Just as women fight sexism and members of ethnic minority groups strive to combat racism, people with mental illness see mentalism as a destructive force.

mental illness themselves. Organizations such as the Mental Patients' Liberation Front (MPLF) applied for grants and opened a series of residences and drop-in crisis centers. In some, patients and professionals work together to provide mental-health services. In others, based on the "separatist model," patients and ex-patients serve as "peer counselors" and run the entire program. Professionals are strictly excluded because they are thought to have "mentalist" attitudes.

Consciousness-raising is a key element of the mental-patients' movement. Judi Chamberlin, a New York activist, describes her powerful connection with other ex-patients:

> We talked about our experiences and discovered how similar they were. Whether we had been in grim state hospitals or expensive private ones, whether we were there voluntarily or involuntarily, whether we had been called schizophrenic, manic depressive, or whatever, our histories had been extraordinarily similar. We had experienced depersonalization, the stupefying effects of drugs, the contempt of those who supposedly "cared" for us. Out of this growing awareness came a deeper understanding of the true purpose of the mental-health system. It is primarily a method of social control.[5]

Despite its anger toward the mental-health system and its mistrust of professionals, the mental-patients' movement has a positive thrust. Activists warn patients not to see themselves as victims of society or of their own illnesses. They emphasize that each individual must take responsibility and work to change his or her life. In most of the work they do, peer counselors encourage others to be proactive. "What I do is to teach people how to do things," states one peer counselor, John Hood. "I do a public speaking group. I do a meeting skills group. It teaches people things. I teach people to take responsibility for their actions. That's good."[6]

In 1990, the Americans with Disabilities Act (ADA) promised an end to discrimination for disabled people in the United States. The bill considers mental illness to be a disability, and accords people with psychiatric disorders the same protection offered to wheelchair-users, blind people, and others with physical impairments. The ADA and the mental-patients' movement signal a new way of looking at mental illness. Instead of thinking of themselves as "sick" or "cured," people with mental disorders are coming to see themselves as living with a disability. It poses some limitations, but one can live with it by accepting its presence and finding ways to adapt. It is not an invasive disease, but part of the person himself. "I still hear voices," one patient explains. "But what I discovered is that it's complicated. . . . It's taken me thirty years to not take medication. It's been difficult, but I have a life. . . . I think of mental illness now as a life situation, kind of an extension of [the grieving process]."

The mental-patients' movement lost one of its most articulate members, Ken Steele, in 2000. Steele had lived with schizophrenia from the age of fourteen. He was in and out of hospitals from New York to California, and spent years homeless on the streets. Finally, when he was forty-six years old, Steele met a therapist who truly believed he could take control of his life. With her support, and with the help of a new antipsychotic medication called clozapine, Steele gained mastery over himself. He became a resource for other psychiatric survivors, and strove to reshape the public's image of people with mental illness. Steele's riveting account of his experiences, *The Day the Voices Stopped*, was published a year after his death. In the Foreword Dr. Stephen Goldfinger writes: "Ken is a classic American hero battling adversity, but the impediments he overcomes are within himself. His strength and his foibles, his rage and his courage, and finally his tenacity and dedication force us to confront ourselves and our world in a new light and with a new empathy."[7]

There are countless heroes in the long and painful history of the mentally ill. Ken Steele is one of millions of people, people of all ages and from every walk of life, who have battled the adversities of severe mental illness. For centuries mental illness was a scourge that turned ordinary people into outcasts. Today, with more effective treatments and a deeper knowledge of brain disorders, people with these conditions can live fuller, more rewarding lives than ever before. Gradually we are chipping away at society's fear and misunderstanding, reducing the stigma of severe mental illness. And for the first time, psychiatric survivors themselves are stepping forward together, speaking out and making their voices heard. As one former patient declared, "We are people, not diagnoses."[8] As we think about the history of people with mental illness, may we recognize their humanity and honor their strength.

CHAPTER ONE

1. Michael Winerip, *9 Highland Road* (New York: Pantheon, 1994), p. 286.
2. World Health Organization, "Mental Health: New Understanding, New Hope" Introduction. 2001.
3. Jay Neugeboren, *Transforming Madness: New Lives for People Living with Mental Illness* (New York: Morrow, 1999), p. 66.
4. Neugeboren, p. 120.

CHAPTER TWO

1. Walter Bromberg, *From Shaman to Psychotherapist: A History of the Treatment of Mental Illness* (Chicago: Henry Regnery, 1975), p. 7.
2. Michael H. Stone, *Healing the Mind: A History of Psychotherapy from Antiquity to the Present* (New York: W. W. Norton, 1997), p. 10.
3. Stanley W. Jackson, *Care of the Psyche: A History of Psychological Healing* (New Haven: Yale University Press, 1999), p. 24.
4. Dale Peterson, ed., *A Mad People's History of Madness* (Pittsburgh: University of Pittsburgh Press, 1982), p. 342.
5. Peterson, p. 341.
6. Peterson, p. 4.
7. Stone, p. 20.

CHAPTER THREE

1. William Shakespeare, *King Lear*, Act III, Scene 4.

2. Walter Bromberg, *From Shaman to Psychotherapist: A History of the Treatment of Mental Illness* (Chicago: Henry Regnery, 1975), p. 41.
3. Bromberg, p. 23.
4. Dale Peterson, ed., *A Mad People's History of Madness* (Pittsburgh, PA: University of Pittsburgh Press, 1982), p. 24.
5. Peterson, p. 8.
6. Ken Steele and Claire Berman, *The Day the Voices Stopped: A Schizophrenic's Journey from Madness to Hope* (New York: Basic Books, 2001), p. 1.
7. Peterson, p. 14.
8. Thomas S. Szasz, *The Manufacture of Madness: A Comparative Study of the Inquisition and the Mental Health Movement* (New York: Harper & Row, 1970), p. 8.
9. Michael H. Stone, *Healing the Mind: A History of Psychotherapy from Antiquity to the Present* (New York: W. W. Norton, 1997), p. 27.
10. Stone, p. 28.
11. Szasz, p. 30.

CHAPTER FOUR

1. Thomas S. Szasz, *The Manufacture of Madness: A Comparative Study of the Inquisition and the Mental Health Movement* (New York: Harper & Row, 1970), p. 14.
2. Michel Foucault, *Madness and Civilization: A History of Insanity in the Age of Reason* (New York: Random House, 1965), p. 39.
3. Foucault, p. 40.

4. Foucault, p. 70.
5. Foucault, p. 71.
6. Foucault, p. 73.
7. Dale Peterson, ed., *A Mad People's History of Madness* (Pittsburgh: University of Pittsburgh Press, 1982), p. 41.
8. Foucault, p. 86.
9. Tracy Thompson, *The Beast: A Reckoning with Depression* (New York: G. P. Putnam's Sons, 1995), p. 3.
10. Michael H. Stone, *Healing the Mind: A History of Psychotherapy from Antiquity to the Present* (New York: W. W. Norton, 1997), p. 41.
11. Stone, p. 41.
12. Stone, p. 43.
13. Edward Shorter, *A History of Psychiatry, from the Era of the Asylum to the Age of Prozac* (New York: John Wiley and Sons, 1997), p. 21.
14. Foucault, p. 242.
15. Foucault, p. 196.
16. Richard Hunter and Ida McAlpin, *Three Hundred Years of Psychiatry: 1535-1860* (New York: Oxford University Press, 1963), p. 266.
17. Andrew Scull, ed. *Madhouses, Mad Doctors, and Madmen: A Social History of Psychiatry in the Victorian Era* (Philadelphia: University of Pennsylvania Press, 1981), p. 38.
18. Peterson, p. 60.
19. David Gollaher, *A Voice for the Mad: The Life of Dorothea Dix* (New York: Free Press, 1995), p. 110.

CHAPTER FIVE

1. Michel Foucault, *Madness and Civilization: A History of Insanity in the Age of Reason* (New York: Random House, 1965), p. 258.

2. Edward Shorter, *A History of Psychiatry, from the Era of the Asylum to the Age of Prozac* (New York: John Wiley and Sons, 1997), p. 8.
3. Foucault, p. 247.
4. Shorter, p. 250.
5. Shorter, p. 19.
6. Shorter, p. 245.
7. Foucault, p. 267.
8. David Gollaher, *A Voice for the Mad: The Life of Dorothea Dix* (New York: Free Press, 1995), p. 148.
9. Gollaher, p. 148.
10. Paul K. Longmore and Lauri Umansky, eds., *The New Disability History: American Perspectives* (New York: New York University Press, 2001), p. 38.
11. Gerald N. Grob, *The Mad Among Us: The History of the Care of America's Mentally Ill* (New York: Free Press, 1994), p. 83.
12. Grob, p. 85.
13. Grob, p. 92.
14. Albert Deutsch, *The Mentally Ill in the United States: A History of Their Care from Colonial Times* (New York: Columbia University Press, 1949), p. 221.
15. Deutsch, p. 222.
16. Dale Peterson, ed., *A Mad People's History of Madness* (Pittsburgh: University of Pittsburgh Press), 1982, p. 134.

CHAPTER SIX

1. C. Peter Bankart, *Talking Cures: A History of Western and Eastern Psychotherapies* (Brooks/Cole, 1997), p. 52.
2. Bankart, p. 86.
3. Stanley W. Jackson, *Care of the Psyche: A History of Psychological Healing* (New Haven: Yale University Press, 1999), p. 107.

4. Bankart, p. 108.
5. Bankart, p. 136.
6. Jackson, p. 107.

CHAPTER SEVEN

1. Clifford W. Beers, *A Mind That Found Itself: An Autobiography* (New York: Doubleday, 1953), p. 41.
2. Beers, p. 129.
3. Michael H. Stone, *Healing the Mind: A History of Psychotherapy from Antiquity to the Present* (New York: W. W. Norton, 1997), p. 156.
4. Jeffrey L. Geller and Maxine Harris, eds., *Women of the Asylum: Voices from behind the Walls, 1840–1945* (New York: Anchor, 1993), p. 255.
5. Geller and Harris, p. 277.
6. Peter Wyden, *Conquering Schizophrenia: A Father, His Son, and a Medical Breakthrough* (New York: Alfred A. Knopf, 1998), p. 117.
7. Wyden, p. 322.
8. Edward Shorter, *A History of Psychiatry, from the Era of the Asylum to the Age of Prozac* (John Wiley & Sons, 1997), p. 209.
9. Shorter, p. 221.
10. Shorter, p. 221.
11. Janine Grobe, ed., *Beyond Bedlam: Contemporary Women Psychiatric Survivors Speak Out* (Chicago: Third Side Press, 1999), p. 192.
12. Mary Jane Ward, *The Snake Pit* (New York: Random House, 1946), p. 238.
13. Wyden, p. 62.

CHAPTER EIGHT

1. Peter Wyden, *Conquering Schizophrenia: A Father, A Son, and a Medical Breakthrough* (New York: Alfred A. Knopf, 1998), p. 69.
2. Edward Shorter, *A History of Psychiatry, from the Era of the Asylum to the Age of Prozac* (New York: John Wiley & Sons), p. 253.
3. Shorter, p. 253.
4. Shorter, p. 255.
5. Wyden, p. 70.
6. Kay Redfield Jamison, *An Unquiet Mind* (New York: Alfred A. Knopf, 1995), p. 3.
7. Shorter, p. 258.
8. Shorter, p. 260.
9. T. M. Luhrmann, *Of Two Minds: An Anthropologist Looks at American Psychiatry* (New York: Vintage, 2001), p. 217.
10. Shorter, p. 254.

CHAPTER NINE

1. Erving Goffman, *Asylums: Essays on the Social Situation of Mental Patients and Other Inmates* (New York: Anchor/Doubleday, 1961), p. 14.
2. Ken Kesey, *One Flew over the Cuckoo's Nest* (New York: Viking, 1962), p. 20.
3. Thomas S. Szasz, *The Manufacture of Madness: A Comparative Study of the Inquisition and the Mental Health Movement* (New York: Harper & Row, 1970), p. 35.
4. R.D. Laing, *The Politics of Experience* (New York: Random House, 1967), p. 127.

5. Mary Barnes and Joseph Berke, *Mary Barnes: Two Accounts of Madness* (New York: Ballantine, 1971), p. 3.

6. Edward Shorter, *A History of Psychiatry, from the Era of the Asylum to the Age of Prozac* (New York: John Wiley and Sons, 1997), p. 277.

7. Szasz, p. 17.

8. Hannah Greene, *I Never Promised You a Rose Garden* (New York: Holt, Rinehart and Winston, 1964), p. 21.

9. Quoted on *60 Minutes*, CBS, March 31, 2002.

10. E. Fuller Torrey, *Nowhere to Go: The Tragic Odyssey of the Homeless Mentally Ill* (New York: Harper & Row, 1988), p. xiv.

11. Torrey, p. 4.

12. Torrey, p. 2.

13. Torrey, p. 23.

14. Michael Winerip, *9 Highland Road* (New York: Pantheon, 1994), p. 2.

15. Kenneth Donaldson, *Insanity Inside Out* (New York: Crown, 1976), p. 327.

16. Donaldson, p. 329.

17. Torrey, p. 33.

CHAPTER TEN

1. Lauren Slater, *Welcome to My Country* (New York: Random House, 1996), p. 103.

2. Jay Neugeboren, *Transforming Madness: New Lives for People Living with Mental Illness* (New York: Morrow, 1999), p. 145.

3. Neugeboren, p. 22.

4. Press Release, National Alliance for the Mentally Ill, Dec. 18, 2001, www.nami.org.

5. Judi Chamberlin, *On Our Own: Patient-Controlled Alternatives to the Mental Health System* (London: MIND, 1976), p. 72.

6. T. M. Luhrmann, *Of Two Minds: An Anthropologist Looks at American Psychiatry* (New York: Vintage, 2001), p. 292.

7. Ken Steele and Claire Berman, *The Day the Voices Stopped: A Schizophrenic's Journey from Madness to Hope* (New York: Basic Books, 2001), p. viii.

8. Steele and Berman, p. 291.

·FOR FURTHER INFORMATION·

GENERAL REFERENCES

Andreasen, Nancy C. *Brave New Brain: Conquering Mental Illness in the Era of the Genome.* New York: Oxford University Press, 2001.

Bromberg, Walter. *From Shaman to Psychotherapist: A History of the Treatment of Mental Illness.* Chicago: Henry Regnery, 1975.

Foucault, Michel. *Madness and Civilization: A History of Insanity in the Age of Reason.* New York: Random House, 1965.

Geller, Jeffrey L., and Maxine Harris. *Women of the Asylum: Voices from behind the Walls, 1840–1945.* New York: Anchor, 1993.

Glenn, Michael, ed. *Voices from the Asylum.* New York: Harper & Row, 1974.

Goffman, Erving. *Asylums: Essays on the Situation of Mental Patients and Other Inmates.* New York: Doubleday/Anchor, 1961.

Gollaher, David. *A Voice for the Mad: A Life of Dorothea Dix.* New York: Free Press, 1995.

Grob, Gerald N. *The Mad Among Us: A History of the Care of America's Mentally Ill.* New York: Free Press, 1994.

Jamison, Kay Redfield. *Touched with Fire: Manic-Depressive Illness and the Artistic Temperament.* New York: Free Press, 1993.

Luhrmann, T. M. *Of Two Minds: An Anthropologist Looks at American Psychiatry.* New York: Vintage, 2001.

Neugeboren, Jay. *Transforming Madness: New Lives for People Living with Mental Illness.* New York: Morrow, 1999.

Peterson, Dale, ed. *A Mad People's History of Madness.* Pittsburgh: University of Pittsburgh Press, 1982.

Slater, Lauren. *Welcome to My Country.* New York: Random House, 1996.

Solomon, Andrew. *The Noonday Demon: An Atlas of Depression.* New York: Scribner's, 2001.

Szasz, Thomas S. *The Manufacture of Madness: A Comparative Study of the Inquisition and the Mental Health Movement.* New York: Harper & Row, 1970.

Torrey, E. Fuller. *Nowhere to Go: The Tragic Odyssey of the Homeless Mentally Ill.* New York: Harper and Row, 1988.

Whitaker, Robert. *Mad in America: Bad Medicine, Bad Science, and the Enduring Mistreatment of the Mentally Ill.* New York: Perseus, 2002.

Winerip, Michael. *9 Highland Road.* New York: Pantheon, 1994.

MEMOIR AND FICTION

Aldrin, Edwin E., with Wayne Warga. *Back to Earth.* New York: Random House, 1973.

Barnes, Mary, and Joseph Berke. *Mary Barnes: Two Accounts of Madness.* New York: Ballantine, 1971.

Beers, Clifford W. *A Mind that Found Itself: An Autobiography.* Garden City, NY: Doubleday, 1953.

Benziger, Barbara. *The Prison of My Mind.* New York: Walker, 1969.

Bottoms, Greg. *Angelhead: My Brother's Descent into Madness.* New York: Crown, 2001.

Donaldson, Kenneth. *Insanity Inside Out.* New York: Crown, 1976.

Farmer, Frances. *Will There Really Be a Morning?* New York: G. P. Putnam's Sons, 1972.

Greene, Hannah. *I Never Promised You a Rose Garden.* New York: Holt, Rinehart and Winston, 1964.

Jamison, Kay Redfield. *An Unquiet Mind.* New York: Alfred A. Knopf, 1995.

Kaysen, Susanna. *Girl, Interrupted.* New York: Turtle Bay/Random House, 1993.

Kesey, Ken. *One Flew over the Cuckoo's Nest.* New York: Viking, 1962.

Logan, Joshua. *Josh: My Up and Down, In and Out Life.* New York: Delacorte, 1976.

Nasar, Sylvia. *A Beautiful Mind: The Life of Mathematical Genius and Nobel Laureate John Nash.* New York: Simon & Schuster, 1994.

Neugeboren, Jay. *Imagining Robert: My Brother, Madness, and Survival.* New York: William Morrow, 1997.

Rubin, Theodore I. *Lisa and David.* New York: Macmillan, 1961.

Schreiber, Flora Rheta. *Sybil.* New York: Warner Books, 1973.

Sechehay, Marguerite. *Autobiography of a Schizophrenic Girl.* New York: New American Library, 1970.

Steele, Ken, and Claire Berman. *The Day the Voices Stopped: A Schizophrenic's Journey from Madness to Hope.* New York: Basic Books, 2001.

Thompson, Tracy. *The Beast: A Reckoning with Depression.* New York: G. P. Putnam's Sons, 1995.

Ward, Mary Jane. *The Snake Pit.* New York: Random House, 1946.

Wyden, Peter. *Conquering Schizophrenia: A Father, His Son, and a Medical Breakthrough.* New York: Alfred A. Knopf, 1998.

ONLINE RESOURCES

American Academy of Child and Adolescent Psychiatry, www.aacap.org.
Help to families of children with psychiatric problems.

American Journal of Psychiatry, www.ajp.psychiatryonline.org.
Official journal of the American Psychiatric Association.

Center for the Advancement of Children's Mental Health, www.kidsmentalhealth.org/

Child and Adolescent Bipolar Foundation, www.bpkids.org.

The Infinite Mind, www.theinfinitemind.com/
Online public radio broadcasts about mental health, the mind, and brain research.

National Alliance for the Mentally Ill, www.nami.org.
News stories and political information related to people with mental illnesses.

National Institute of Mental Health, www.nimh.nih.gov/publicat/resfacts.cfm.
Provides statistics and information about major mental illnesses.

Schizophrenia Network, www.schizophrenia.com.
Book reviews, news stories, and articles by and about people with schizophrenia.

Substance Abuse and Mental Health Services Administration, www.samhsa.gov/statistics/statistics/html.

Surgeon General's Report on Mental Health, www.surgeongeneral.gov/library/mentalhealth/index/html.

c. 3000 B.C.   Babylonian healers inscribe cure for madness on cuneiform tablets.

c. 2500 B.C.   Egyptian priests treat illnesses, including madness, by inducing "incubation sleep."

c. 1400 B.C.   Hindus establish the first known asylums for mentally ill persons.

c. 400 B.C.   Hippocrates suggests theory of four humors to explain illness.

c. 300 B.C.   Plato writes that the brain is the seat of the "rational soul."

c. 180 A.D.   Galen writes that the nerves carry messages between the brain and other parts of the body.

c. 300   The Christian Church discourages scientific inquiry into anatomy; prescribes faith as the only healer.

c. 850   Unhammad describes a variety of psychiatric conditions, including paranoia and obsessive-compulsive disorder (OCD).

c. 1020   Avicenna compiles medical encyclopedia describing several kinds of mental disorders.

c. 1190   Maimonides writes about mental illness and moral imbalance.

1329   St. Mary of Bethlehem Priory in London opens its doors to the poor and insane.

1403   St. Mary of Bethlehem is turned into a madhouse, known as Bedlam.

1484   Pope Innocent VIII issues a Papal Bull, calling upon the church to eradicate witches.

1486   Heinrich Kramer and James Sprenger publish the *Malleus Maleficarum*, a book explaining how witches can be identified.

1621 Robert Burton publishes *The Anatomy of Melancholy*, a book about depression.

1656 King Louis XIII founds the Hôpital Géneral in Paris to care for the poor and the insane.

1728 Daniel Defoe protests abuses by private madhouses, especially those that incarcerate unwanted wives.

1774 Anton Mesmer goes to Paris and popularizes the notion of "animal magnetism."

1788 King George III of England has the first of several attacks of madness.

1793 Philippe Pinel unchains twelve male patients in the Bicêtre Hospital in Paris.

1796 William Tuke opens the York Retreat in England.

1842 Dorothea Dix pleads with the Massachusetts legislature for better treatment of the mentally ill.

1843 British courts rule that Daniel McNaughton is not guilty of murder on the grounds that he was insane when he committed the act.

1872 Jean-Martin Charcot presents his theory of hypnotism to the Academy of Sciences in Paris.

1895 Sigmund Freud and Josef Breuer publish their findings on the case of "Anna O."

1899 Freud publishes *The Interpretation of Dreams*.

1908 Clifford Beers publishes *A Mind that Found Itself* and launches the mental-hygiene movement.

1911 A rift occurs between Freud and two of his most gifted followers, Alfred Adler and Carl Jung; Eugen Bleuler coins the term *schizophrenia*.

1934 Doctors in the United States pioneer the use of insulin-shock therapy.

1938 Ugo Cerletti uses electric shock to treat a psychotic man in Rome.

1946 Mary Jane Ward publishes her autobiographical novel *The Snake Pit*.

1949 Egas Moniz receives the Nobel Prize for his development of prefrontal lobotomy.

1952 Henri Laborit suggests that a new drug, chlorpromazine, may be effective with psychiatric patients; the first edition of the *Diagnostic and Statistical Manual of Mental Disorders* is published.

1955 Imipramine is developed to combat depression.

1960 R. D. Laing publishes his theory on schizophrenia in *The Divided Self*; Thomas Szasz publishes *The Myth of Mental Illness*.

1963 President John F. Kennedy launches the community mental-health movement.

1970 The U.S. government approves lithium for treatment of manic-depressive illness.

1975 The U.S. Supreme Court rules that the state cannot hold a non-dangerous person without providing treatment.

1994 John Forbes Nash Jr., who had been diagnosed with schizophrenia, wins the Nobel Prize.

2001 Mental-health advocates lobby Congress for legislation that would create parity between physical and mental illnesses for insurance coverage.

·GLOSSARY·

Animal magnetism—the eighteenth-century concept of a magnetic fluid from the sky that influenced the health of all living things.

Autism—a condition that begins in early childhood, characterized by poor language skills, difficulty relating to others, and endlessly repetitive activities such as spinning objects or flicking light switches.

Bipolar disorder (also called manic-depressive illness)—a mental illness in which a person's moods cycle from manic heights to pits of severe depression.

Delusion—a false but compelling idea based on a misinterpretation of reality. Delusions of grandeur or persecution are among the most common.

Hallucination—the perception of a sound, smell, person, or object that does not exist in reality.

Hypnotism—the practice of inducing a trance and gaining access to the unconscious mind.

Hysteria—a condition in which unconscious feelings and conflicts produce symptoms such as tremors, paralysis, or blindness; these symptoms have no physiological basis.

Incubation sleep—drug-induced sleep used in ancient Egypt and Greece for the treatment of illness, including madness.

Incubi and succubi—devils thought to invade men and women during sleep.

Mania—a frenzied state of high energy, intense activity, and grandiose thinking.

Melancholia—an early term for depression.

Mood disorder—the group of mood-related conditions including bipolar disorder and unipolar depression.

Neurology—the branch of medicine concerned with the treatment of diseases of the nervous system.

Neurosis—any of several relatively mild psychiatric disorders, in which a person may have minor depression, phobias, anxiety, or other problems, but maintains strong contact with reality.

Obsessive-compulsive disorder—a mental illness in which a person has inescapable obsessive thoughts or uncontrollable compulsions to perform an action again and again.

Panic attack—a sudden attack of intense anxiety or terror, accompanied by physical symptoms such as panting, sweating, increased heart rate, and dizziness.

Paranoia—the delusion that one is being persecuted by others. Paranoia sometimes occurs in schizophrenia or in manic states.

Phobia—an intense fear of an object or situation that is not dangerous in reality.

Psychiatry—the branch of medicine concerned with the treatment of mental illness.

Psychoanalysis—the method of intensive psychotherapy that attempts to uncover unconscious memories and conflicts.

Psychosis—a state of mind in which a person loses touch with reality; schizophrenia and severe mood disorders can lead to psychotic states.

Schizophrenia—a severe form of mental illness, usually beginning in adolescence, characterized by disorganized thinking and poor contact with reality.

Trepanning—the ancient practice of drilling holes in the skull, perhaps to release evil spirits.

Unconscious mind—mental activity that occurs below the conscious level, and may be expressed in dreams and behavior.

Unipolar depression—a mood disorder characterized by profound sadness, hopelessness, and lack of interest in life.

·INDEX·

Page numbers in *italics* refer to illustrations.